Introduction

The Essentials of GCSE ICT is suitable for use by students studying any of the major exam board specifications for Information and Communication Technology.

The guide contains everything you need to know for your GCSE ICT exam, with advice on how to approach your coursework.

It covers the core components of the course, including the structure of information systems, components and peripherals, networks and communications, operating system software, applications software, system design, and the role and implications of information systems in society.

The guide is divided into six easy to follow sections to help you revise for the exam in a logical order. Taking time to study the glossary at the back of the book will also aid your understanding of the essentials of GCSE ICT.

The author, Eric Deeson, is an expert in the field of Information and Communication Technology, with over 40 years' experience of teaching and training. He has taught in a number of schools and colleges, as Head of Computing and Director of Resources and IT, and now runs a successful education and training consultancy. He has written a number of publications on information and communication systems and their applications.

With special thanks to Beckie Woollett, Bridget Parsons, Mark Reader, Matthew Griffiths, Peter Gregory and Ric Deeson.

The author and publisher would also like to thank everyone who contributed images to this book:

- AOL (UK) Ltd
- Clarkson University, Potsdam, USA
- Global Robots Ltd
- ICI Dulux
- Scripture Union (www.livewires.org.uk)
- Telford & Shropshire Marketing Partnership
- The Yorkshire Flight Centre
- Zen Internet

Screen shots reprinted by permission from Microsoft Corporation

Contents

Contents

What is ICT?

Communications

Software & Applications

System Design

Describing Data

ICT in Society

What is a Computer?

These two pages cover...

- **information systems in terms of hardware blocks and data flows**
- **information and data**
- **hardware**

ICT Systems

Information and communication technology refers to computers and a range of other devices that behave like computers. We call these items **information systems**. All information systems process data.

The photos on the left show some examples of information systems. There are thousands of others, ranging from large mainframe computers to small **microprocessors** used in household equipment such as washing machines and DVD players.

Other examples of information systems include a laptop, a car's navigation system, a 3-D radar display, a digital radio and a central heating control unit.

So what do they all have in common? What makes them information systems?

Information System Hardware

We can look at all information systems as being made up of five basic building blocks with flows of data between them, as shown in the diagram alongside.

It is important that you understand this diagram and that you know which parts of a computer (or other information system) relate to each building block.

Compare the diagram with the desktop computer (below right).

The computer's main box includes both the **processor** (on the 'motherboard') and the **main store**; these two parts are in the **central processing unit (CPU)**. All the other parts are **peripherals**. The peripherals connect to the main box. However, if the peripheral **backing store** is a disk drive (as is normal for computers), then it is likely to be in the main box too.

It's common to have more than one **input unit** such as a keyboard and mouse, and more than one **output unit** such as a screen and printer.

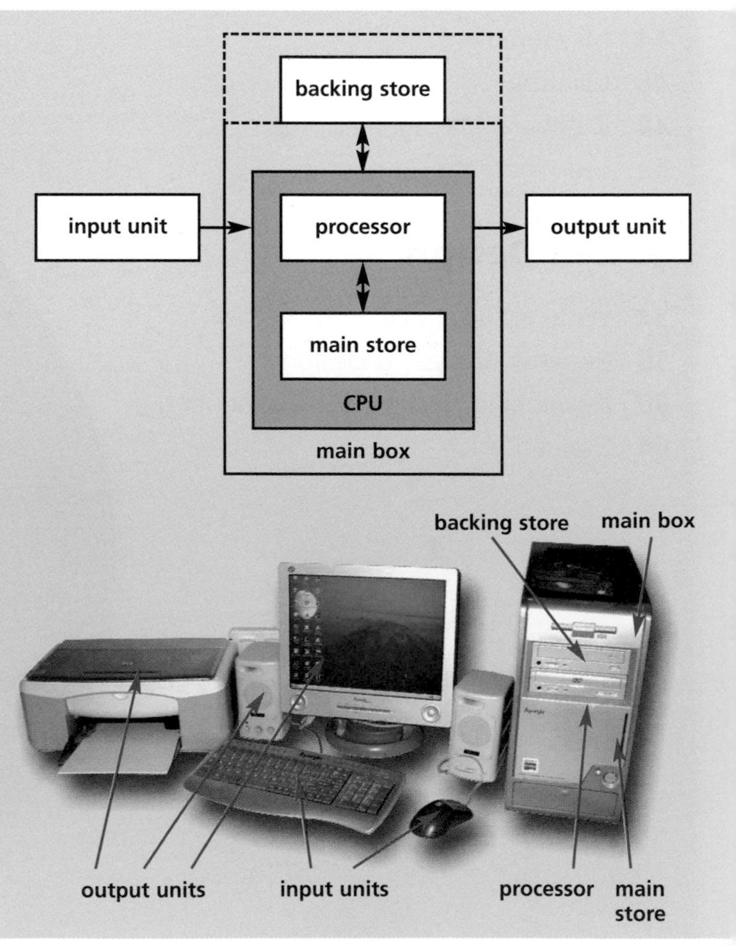

Information v Data

There is a difference between information and data: information has meaning but data does not.

The picture above shows some numbers. What do they mean to you? Nothing. They have no context so they are meaningless and are therefore an example of data.

However if you turn the paper over and see 'my bank PIN', the data suddenly gains meaning and becomes information.

What goes on inside an information system is, in fact, data handling not information handling. Machines have no intelligence so what goes on inside them has no meaning.

When you enter information into an information system, for example, typing text into a computer through a keyboard, it instantly becomes data. After processing, the computer sends data to the output unit (screen) and when you read it, it makes sense so is now information.

Hardware

The five blocks in the diagram on the facing page are hardware, which means they are solid units (i.e. bits you can touch).

The central processing unit (CPU)...

- is a hugely complex electronic circuit
- consists of the processor plus the main store
- is the core of any information system.

The processor (part of the CPU)...

- is one or more chips in the CPU
- is a complex circuit that follows instructions in order to handle data in various ways (e.g. transfer it, store it, change it).

The main store (part of the CPU)...

- is a set of chips in the CPU
- holds all the data needed by the processor
- holds the software (see page 7).

The backing store...

- stores the user's data and software so it can be accessed in the future
- may be peripheral or in the main box
- may be a floppy drive, hard drive, CD drive or memory stick.

Peripherals...

- are all the parts outside the CPU, i.e. input units, output units and sometimes the backing store.

Input units...

- take in information from the user, or data from somewhere else (such as a sensor), and pass it on in the form of data to the CPU to be processed
- include, for example, the scanner, keyboard and mouse.

Output units...

- convert data from the CPU into information for the user
- include, for example, the speakers, screen and printer.

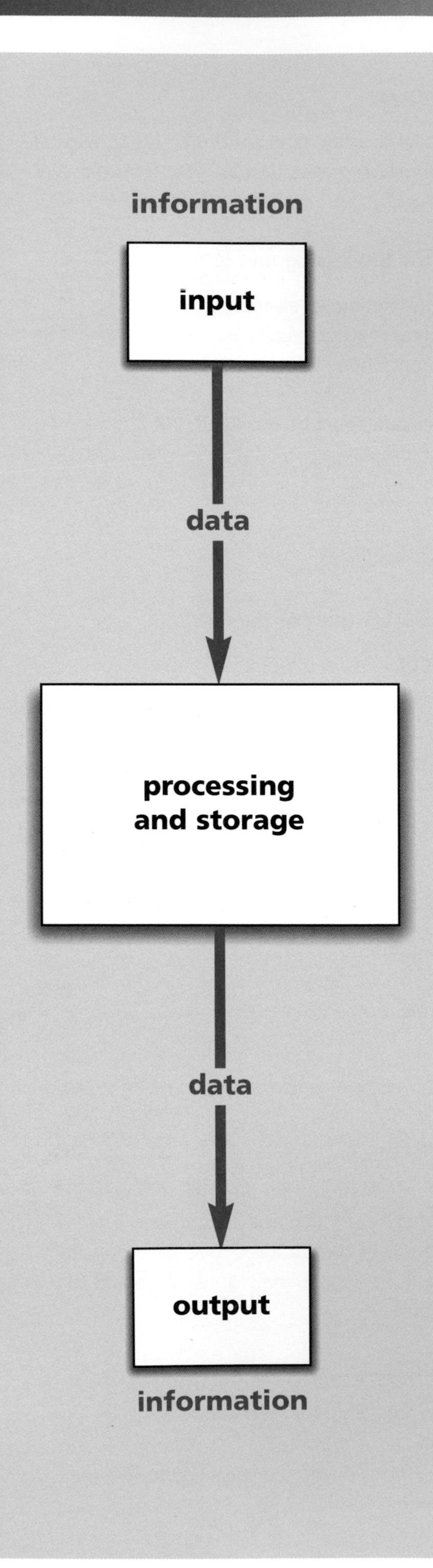

These two pages cover...

- **channels in information systems**
- **the two main types of software**
- **the four main types of computer**

In any information system the hardware is connected by channels or links (shown by arrows in the diagram alongside and in the basic block diagram on page 4). Data flows through these channels, which are mostly metal wires (encased in plastic) but may be radio waves, micro-waves or infra-red.

The diagram alongside shows the flow of data through an information system.

You can describe any information system by outlining what happens at each stage in the diagram.

Using a fax machine as an example...

1. Information on a piece of paper is inserted into the fax machine (input unit).
2. Once inside the machine the information becomes data and travels to the CPU (main store and processor).
3. The data is processed in the CPU.
4. The data leaves the CPU and travels to the receiving fax machine (output unit).
5. A copy is printed out of the receiving fax machine and is once again information.

Fax machine (to send and receive documents)

Mainframe

What is Software?

Software is a type of data. It is data which the information system recognises as instructions. These instructions tell the hardware how to handle the data in the system.

There are two main types of software:

1. **Operating system software** (also known as **system software** or **operating system**). Operating system software runs the hardware without you knowing, or needing to know, what it is doing. It looks after the system, for example, making sure the processor can follow each instruction and that the peripherals do what they should. Without operating system software, an information system cannot work.
2. **Application software.** This software is the programs people actually use when working with computers. You need to know about word processing, spreadsheets, data logging and control, and database management application software.

Handheld
Desktop (PC)
Laptop

The Main Computer Types

There are four main types of computer, as shown here. The mainframe is very powerful and is used by large firms and in advanced science and technology. You will probably recognise the other three: desktop, laptop and handheld.

All computers are data processing machines that are...
Programmable: they use software to tell them what to do, and different software instructs them to do different things.
Digital electronic: they work with small electric currents that have only two values (0 and 1 or OFF and ON)

The box below shows how the four types of computers differ.

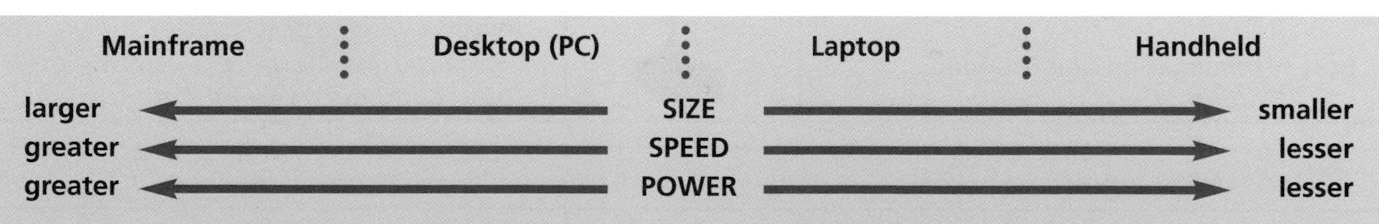

Mainframe	Desktop (PC)	Laptop	Handheld
Large and very costly to buy and run. Used in large offices, labs and workshops for powerful 'number-crunching'. They are usually housed in special air-conditioned rooms and are accessed through workstations.	A stand-alone personal computer (PC) can be used by one person at home, at work or as part of a network. Their peripherals take up a lot of space and they are difficult to move from place to place (especially when networked).	Smaller and lighter than desktops, with integrated screens and compact keyboards. They range from large laptops to small 'notebooks'. Laptops have an hour or more of battery power, so they can be used anywhere.	Also known as palmtops, they are much smaller and easier to carry than laptops but too small for easy prolonged use. Modern handhelds use touch-sensitive screens. Some mobile (cell) phones include this type of computer.

Input Units

These two pages cover...

- **input units for information systems, including keyboards, pointing devices, digitisers, digital cameras and sensors**

Input units are hardware units designed to accept information (or data) and send it to the CPU in the form of data. If you learn all the facts, shown here, you should be able to cope with any exam question on input units. It would also help you to look at, and practise using, as many input units as you can. Exam papers expect you to recognise and to be able to say when you would use each type of input unit.

Keyboards

A keyboard is a device with a number of different keys. Each key has a switch below it which produces its own effect when pressed (i.e. letter, number, symbol etc.).

Pros and Cons

+ we're used to keyboards
– slow, bulky, costly and prone to failure
– can cause repetitive strain injury

Best for inputting text

The **'QWERTY' keyboard** is the standard type (named after the arrangement of the first six letter keys).

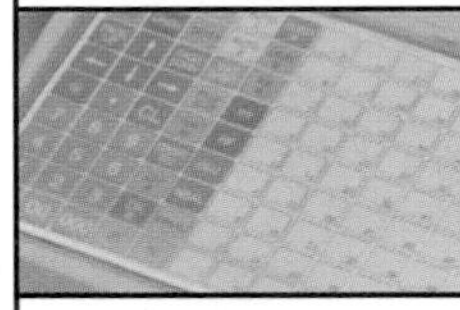

The **concept keyboard** surface has switches you can program to match any overlay (used in restaurants where each key is one item).

Phones, calculators and other special units use **keypads**, in most cases with far fewer keys.

Pointing Devices

A pointing device is able to control the screen cursor by sensing movement or pressure.

Pros and Cons (for mouse)

+ cheap
+ easy and quick to use for most people
+ wireless versions exist
– prone to failure
– fiddly for some
– can cause repetitive strain injury

Best for navigation and drawing

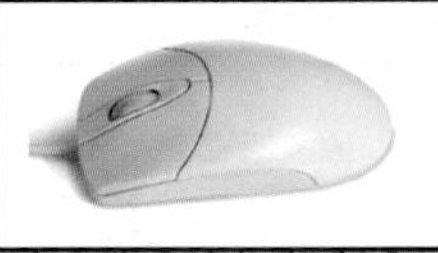

The **mouse** is the standard pointing device. Some laptops have a roller ball – an upside-down mouse that needs less space.

The **touchpad** is now the most common pointing unit for laptops.

Most handhelds use **touch pens**.

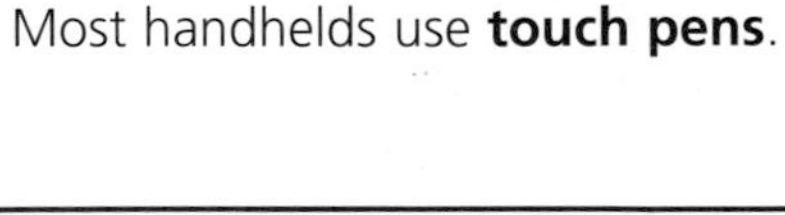

Joysticks (or even more complex pointer units) are used by game players to control the action.

Digitisers

A digitiser is an input unit that changes graphical or analogue input into a form a computer can use, i.e. digital. For example, a graphics pad converts the position of the pen on the surface into digital data.

Pros and Cons

+ very useful in special contexts
– often very costly
– sometimes fiddly

The **graphics pad** (or tablet) is a pressure-sensitive pad and is great for designers.

A **touch screen** is rather like a graphics pad but is on the screen so is easier to use in some contexts.

A **scanner** can convert pictures etc. on paper to digital. **OCR (optical character recognition)** converts scanned text (see page 67).

Digital Cameras

Digital cameras are able to record an image in digital form for later transfer to a processor and / or output unit. The quality of the image depends on the number of pixels. **Pros and Cons** + very useful in special contexts – often very costly (though low-quality webcams are cheap)		The **digital still camera** is for photos (but most can also take video).
		The **digital video camera** is for moving images but most can also take stills.
	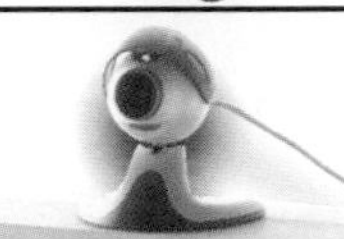	Low-quality **webcams** are used to transmit images through the Internet.

Sensors

Sensor-based input units detect and / or measure energy in one form and produce an electric output (see pages 44-47). **Pros and Cons** + all are good at their job + they are cheap NB. Almost all input units depend on some kind of sensor.		A **microphone** (sound sensor) is the input unit for dictating to a computer (speech recognition) and for phones.
	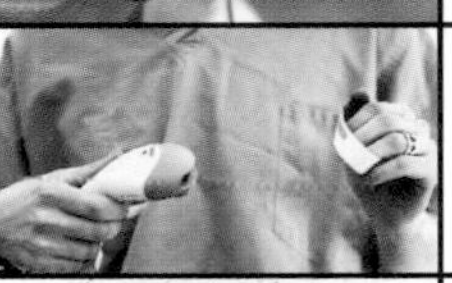	A **light pen** (light sensor) is used to input data, for example, from a barcode.
		**Remote controls** pass signals to sensors in information systems by, for example, infra-red.
		An **optical mark reader (OMR)** contains a lamp and a row of light sensors: OMR software looks for certain marks in certain places, such as on lottery tickets (see page 67).

Look at this set-up. An electronic instrument is an information system: the input unit in this case is the music keyboard. But any electronic instrument with a MIDI (Musical Instrument Digital Interface) output can feed data to a computer that has a MIDI input and software like Sibelius – and thus process the data.

Sibelius Software

MIDI Music Lab

Output Units

These two pages cover...

- **output units for information systems, including screens, printers, plotters, transducers and control systems**

Output units are hardware units that convert the processed data from an information system into a format that the user can understand. As before, it would help you to look at and use as many of these units as you can. For your exam, you should be able to recognise all the main output peripherals and be able to say when you would use each one.

Screens

A screen, monitor or VDU (visual display unit) is the main output unit for computers. It instantly shows what you enter and the system's response. You can control the brightness and colour of the screen. We describe screens by type, size and resolution (number of pixels across and down).

Pros and Cons

+ fast acting; you can see what you want straightaway
- costly
- cathode ray tube (CRT) uses a lot of power and needs high voltage
- CRT could be unhealthy (radiation)
- no 'hard copy' (i.e. no permanent copy)

Best for fast output

The standard **cathode ray tube (CRT)** screen is like an old TV set – bulky controls direct beams of electrons through the vacuum tube from point to point on the back of the screen to build the image.

There are two types of flat screen – **liquid crystal display (LCD)** and **thin-film transistor (TFT**, also known as Matrix). Both are smaller and lighter than CRT screens, but tend to be a bit more expensive.

Printers

Until suitable screens were developed, the printer was the main output unit, producing (originally very slowly) hard copies of the user's inputs and the system's outputs. Printers are now much more efficient. We describe printers by speed (number of pages per minute) and print resolution (number of dots per inch (dpi) or per centimetre).

Pros and Cons

+ produces permanent records (hard copy)
+ some can also be used as a scanner, copier or fax machine
- costly to buy and / or use
- fiddly and unreliable
- consumables, e.g. ink and paper, can be expensive

Best for permanent records

The **dot matrix (or impact) printer** is rare now, except for shop tills and some cash machines. It is the cheapest, but also the slowest and noisiest. Pins in the printhead hit ink from a ribbon onto the paper.

Laser printers work in the same way as photocopiers. They're very fast and quiet and have high resolution. They are expensive to buy but are cheap to run, so they are popular in offices.

The printhead of an **inkjet printer** spurts tiny drops of ink onto paper. Inkjets are fast, quiet, very good for colour and cheaper to buy than laser printers. Inkjets are commonly used with home computers.

Plotters

A plotter can produce a more precise drawing (e.g. for a designer) than a printer and on a larger sheet of paper too. Both types (flatbed and drum) have a number of pens the software moves against the paper in order to produce the drawing. However, printers are slowly taking over from plotters.	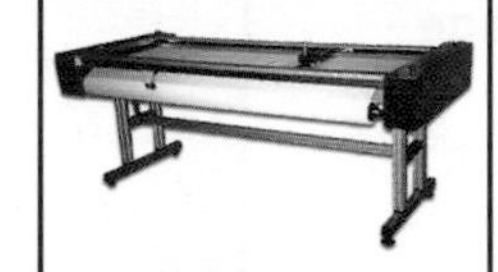	In the **flatbed plotter** the pens move over the paper.
Best for complex drawings 		In the **drum plotter** the paper moves below the pens.

Transducers / Actuators

A transducer is the reverse of a sensor: it converts an input electric current to a mechanical output (an output the user can see / hear / feel).		The (loud) **speaker** is the reverse of the microphone: it changes input current to a matching sound output. Earphones are a quieter version.
Pros and Cons + like sensors, each transducer does its special job very well + transducers are cheap	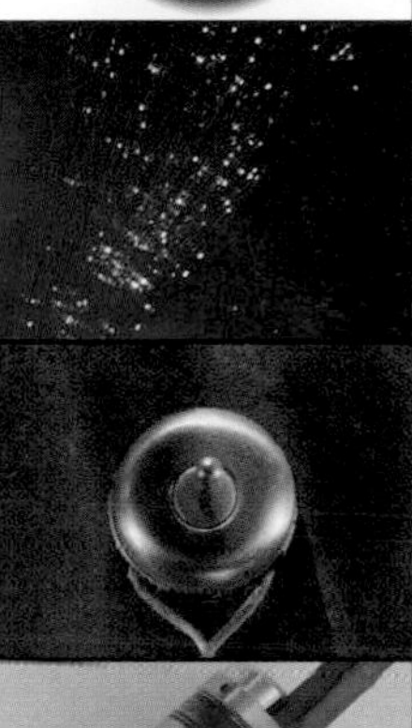	An **LED** (**light-emitting diode**) converts electricity input into the information system into light.
		A **bell** or **buzzer** changes the input current to a sound (output). 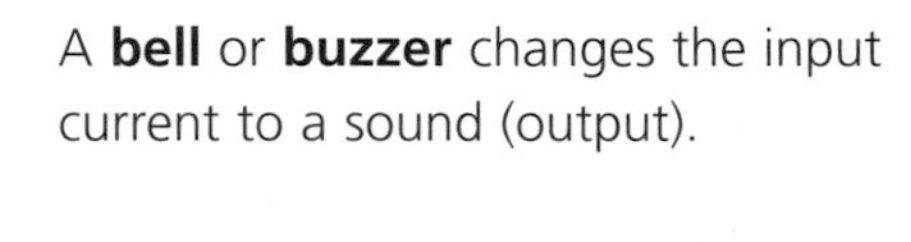
	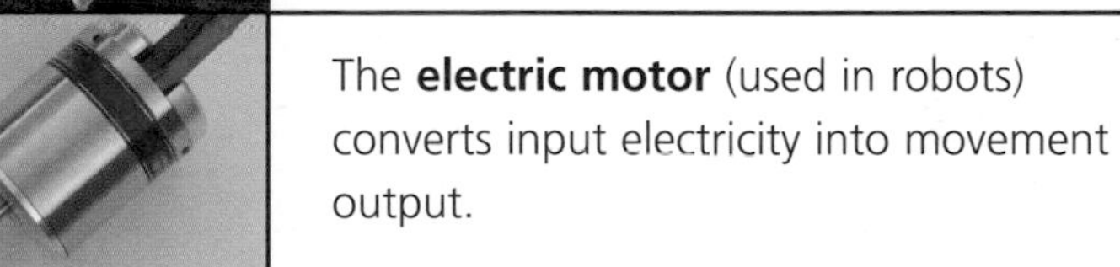	The **electric motor** (used in robots) converts input electricity into movement output.

Control Systems

A control system uses a feedback loop to regulate its output. For example, you can use a computer to control a heater in a room; when the room gets too warm / cold the system switches the heater off / on (see pages 46-47).		A simple **robot** is used to spray paint onto cars. Feedback tells it how close the car's surface is. A motor (see above) moves each part of the robot and sensors feed back its position.
Robots are the most well-known control systems. Under control of software, with feedback as input, they do jobs like painting cars.		A **robotic arm** can be programmed to pick things up and move them around. Feedback tells you where the hand is and how hard it is pressing.
		The **automatic train driver** is a kind of robot; it starts and stops the train and changes speed according to the environment.

Storing Data

These two pages cover...

- **a computer's main store - ROM and RAM**
- **the main types of computer backing storage**

We describe and compare storage types by cost, speed of access to data, and size in megabytes. A megabyte (MB) is about a million characters of text or a high quality photo.

Main Store - ROM and RAM

There are different kinds of storage chip – those that can't hold data when the computer is switched off (volatile) and those that can. We use the latter to store data we always need (e.g. the software for starting a computer after switch-on – operating system software). Of course this kind of data must not change – we mustn't be able to write data to such chips as we would over-write existing data. So these chips are read-only memory (ROM) (memory is another word for storage). But we can write to volatile chips, so they provide read and write memory, RAM (random access memory). RAM holds the data and programs that you are working on at one time.

Backing Store

The backing store is classed as peripheral hardware, although it is sometimes inside the same box as the CPU. It normally takes the form of a hard disk and is used for storing your own data. The following information describes the types of backing store:

Main Store...	Backing Store...
holds the processor's data (you don't have much to do with it)	holds *your* data
is part of the CPU	is peripheral
is always on one or more chips	usually isn't on chips (except for storage stick)
is accessed much faster than backing store (because access to data on chips is faster)	takes longer to access than the main store
tends to be a few hundred megabytes (on desktop computers)	may be tens of thousands of megabytes (tens of gigabytes)

Hard Disks (Magnetic Media)

A hard disk is a stiff magnetic disk (or several on the same axle) in a drive unit with moving heads (the hard drive). The heads can read stored data and write (record) it on the disks. They are the main backing storage for computers and servers.

Pros and Cons

+ high speed of data transfer
+ can store huge volumes of data
+ reliable and secure (if you take care)
– quite costly
– must be backed up

Best for storing lots of data

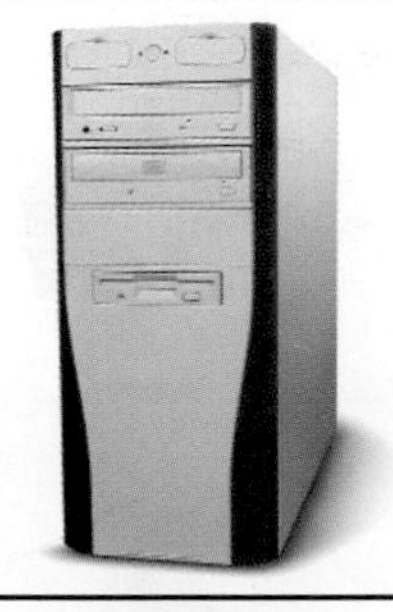

Hard disks are used to store the operating system software and application software. Most **hard disk units** are metal disks coated with a magnetic layer and sealed in a box (drive) with the read / write heads.

Hard disk packs can be removed to keep the data safe or to use it elsewhere. They can be used in place of, or in addition to, fixed hard disk units.

Other Magnetic Media

While hard disks are everywhere now, magnetic tape was the norm for decades. Floppy disks are magnetic too and are now more common than magnetic tape.

Pros and Cons (of tape)

+ can store huge volumes of data
+ good for backing up
- slow
- bulky
- can only access data in sequence (disks offer direct access)

Good for back-up

Magnetic tape works like an audio tape - it stores data files in order. Magnetic tape is more hard wearing than a magnetic disk (e.g. floppy disk) but it takes longer to access information from a magnetic tape.

A **floppy disk** has its magnetic layer on a thin sheet of plastic, so it needs looking after. It is removable and is very popular although storage space is limited (1.4 MB).

A **zip drive** is a portable hard disk unit used for backing up. Zip disks can store a few hundred megabytes.

Optical Media

Data is stored in tiny pits on the surface of the disk, written to and read by a special light-emitting diode (a kind of tiny laser). Various types other than CDs and DVDs have appeared over the years, even optical tape.

Pros and Cons

+ can store huge volumes of data
+ cheap
+ reliable
+ you can write to (record on) some types with the right drives
- need some care in handling

Best for sending out lots of data and for backing up

Compact discs for data are like CDs for music. The standard types are the non-recordable CD-ROM, the CD-R (recordable) and CD-RW (read and write i.e. recordable more than once or 'rewritable'). Each holds up to 700 MB.

The **DVD (digital video / versatile disc)** can store all kinds of digital data, not just video. The capacity of the standard types is 4.7 GB (4700 MB). The types are DVD-ROM (read only), and DVD-RAM, DVD-R, DVD-RW, DVD+R, DVD+RW (recordable / rewritable).

More on Peripherals

Although a backing store, or any input or output unit, is a peripheral within an information system, it is also an information system in itself. Data enters it for processing and leaves after that. Most peripheral units have their own main store too – called a **buffer** – to hold the data in transit. Some units combine both input and output functions quite clearly; here are some you should know:

- **headset** – earphones (output) and microphone (input) in one unit
- **data projector** – projector (output) you can control (input)
- **touch screen** – a screen (output) you can touch to control (input)
- **interactive whiteboard** – like a very large touch screen, often used in classrooms

These two pages cover...

- **the two main types of network - WAN and LAN**
- **the three network topologies (configurations)**
- **the advantages and disadvantages of networks**

All computers and information systems process data, which they *may* convert to / from information. We say 'may' because...

- some information systems are fully automatic and don't involve information at all (e.g. robots whose only inputs are from sensors).
- it's common for information systems to be linked into a network, where the channels carry data out of one system and into the next.

WANs and LANs

Networks are linked information systems between which data can transfer as required under the control of software.

To allow computers to 'talk' to each other, each one must be fitted with a **network interface card**, programmed with a unique address. This ensures the right information goes to the right computer.

The **Internet** is a wide-area network (WAN): the world's biggest network linking millions of computers. You can use a computer to connect to the Internet and obtain information from millions of 'pages' worldwide, email people, play games, plan trips, buy things etc.

School computers are often linked together into an **Intranet**, which is a local-area network (LAN). A LAN lets you share documents between nearby users (e.g. within a school or company), email each other, play games together, print something on a networked printer elsewhere etc.

Network Topologies (Configurations)

Networks can be set up in three different ways, though most combine types:

- the line ('bus') network
- the ring network
- the star network.

Line ('bus') network: Cheapest to install, but unreliable. If the main cable fails, a number of workstations may be affected.

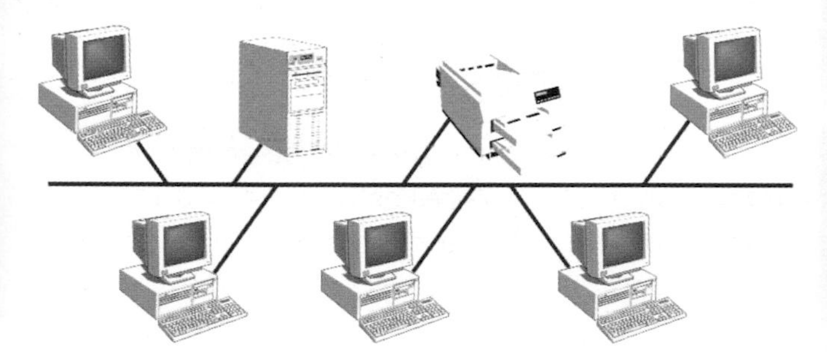

Ring network: Very fast as all data travels in the same direction. Least reliable; if the main cable fails, all workstations are affected.

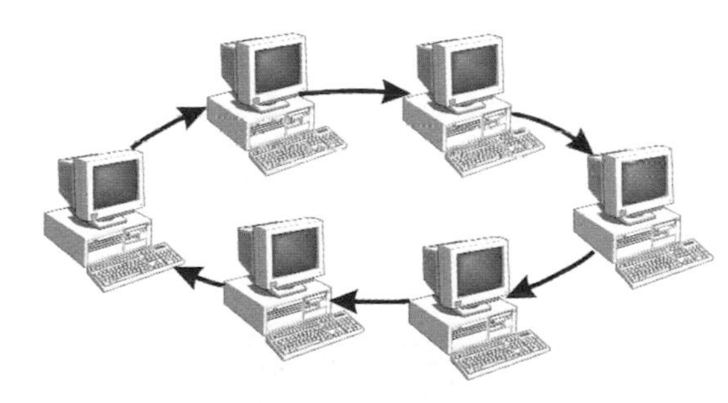

Star network: Most reliable as a failure at one workstation is confined to that workstation. Expensive to install though.

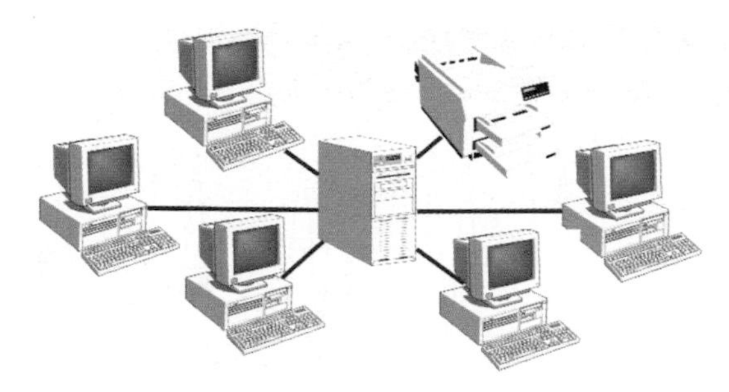

As with anything, the more parts in a system, the greater the chance of faults. The information systems themselves are very reliable – the main problems come from the data transfers between the parts, whether the channels are metal, light fibre, radio or infra-red, and whether the data is analogue or digital.

Advantages and Disadvantages of Networking

Advantages	Disadvantages
People can communicate easily and share information, documents and resources.	Tighter security is needed (from viruses, spam, access to unhealthy sites, over-use of costly hardware etc.).
Saves time and money as peripherals (e.g. printers) can be shared.	High set-up and maintenance costs (often including extra staffing and management e.g. network manager).
Security can be managed centrally (by a network manager who controls what each user has access to).	There's more that can go wrong as networks are complex set-ups, often reliant on one server.

What is Data?

These two pages cover...

- **data flows in an information system**
- **analogue and digital data**
- **bits and bytes**
- **bit patterns**

We started this section by looking at information systems and how data flows through them.

1. Data flows from the input unit to the CPU.
2. The CPU stores the data and processes it to produce more useful data.
3. The data that results flows to the output unit.
4. Software controls all this, and also controls data flows to and from the backing store.

Almost all information systems work with data in digital form.

Analogue and Digital Data

Analogue data is able to take any value in a range, for example, the reading from a pressure sensor.

Digital data is able to take only two values (0 and 1, OFF and ON). However, the great advantage of digital data transfer (communication) is that even if there's lots of noise (interference), you can still detect the 0s and 1s. Software can read digital signals, even very weak ones, for example, from a distant spacecraft.

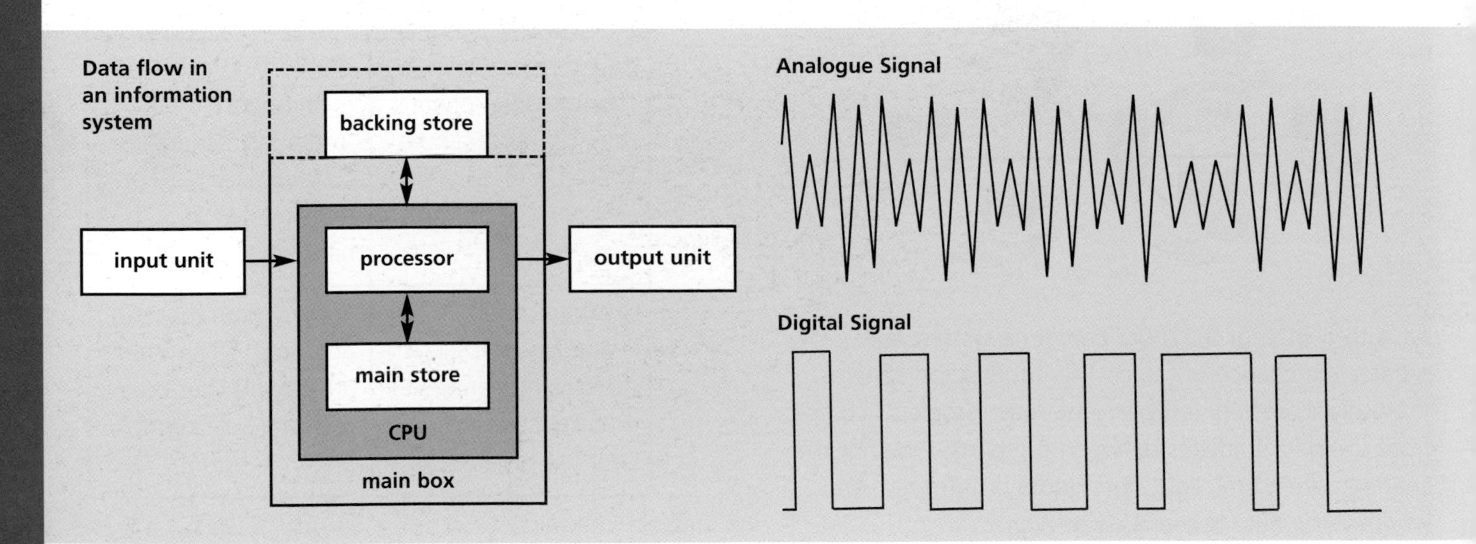

What is Data?

Bits and Bytes

Computers use electricity and process data by using microscopic switches to turn the electrical current on or off. This on / off pattern allows the computer to create signals that correspond to binary digits.

Binary code uses only two digits: 1 (representing ON) and 0 (representing OFF). Therefore a single switch (either ON or OFF) creates a binary digit or 'bit' (the smallest piece of information a computer can process).

Most computers store bits together in groups of eight, known as bytes.

When storing data we refer to the size of a file in terms of bytes:

Bit a binary digit (i.e. 0 or 1)
Byte 8 bits (i.e. a bit pattern)
Kilobyte 1024 bytes
Megabyte 1024 kilobytes
Gigabyte 1024 megabytes

Bit patterns

The bit pattern of a byte produces an eight number binary code. Each digit in a bit pattern represents a number twice the value of the number on its right:

128	64	32	16	8	4	2	1
0	**0**	**1**	**0**	**1**	**1**	**0**	**1**

The value of a bit pattern is calculated by adding together the numbers that are switched ON (i.e. shown as 1). So if a bit pattern is shown as 00101101 (see diagram above), work out 1+ 4 + 8 + 32 to give the value 45.

Each character on a keyboard is represented by a 1 byte ASCII code. So the letter R = ASCII code 82 = bit pattern 01010010. Other examples are shown in the table below. (If you hold ALT down on your PC keyboard and type in the ASCII code, the corresponding character will appear on screen).

Character	ASCII Code	Bit Pattern
%	**37**	**00100101**
2	**50**	**00110010**
g	**103**	**01100111**
M	**77**	**01001101**

ASCII (American Standard Code for Information Interchange) is the standard code for the character sets used in most computers. However, ASCII only uses the lower seven bits of each byte to create a basic character set (i.e. basic controls, numbers, unaccented letters in upper/lower case etc.).

Modern coded character sets such as Unicode (a 16-bit character set) provide extensions to ASCII by using values above 127 to create expanded character sets including letters with accents.

With suitable software to code and de-code bytes, a byte can stand for any kind of information: a sound, some music, a graphic, a program instruction etc.

Basic Communications

These two pages cover...

- **how information and data differ in the context of communication**
- **systems for the transfer of information and digital data**
- **data transfer speeds**
- **phone networks**

Communication

Communication used to mean the transfer of information (knowledge) between people. Now it also refers to the transfer of digital data through information systems. Here are some scenarios where you may need to communicate (think how you would deal with each and how your grandparents would have dealt with them at your age):

- Your younger brother has to learn how to lay the table for dinner.
- Your older sister is still asleep, everyone else is out, and you need to let her know you're going out.
- You want to tell your friend at home you're having a great holiday in France.
- You're having problems with your maths homework and you want your friend to help.

When your grandparents were young, people often went to visit each other and used the postal service a lot. We still tend to speak face-to-face to people we live with, or leave written notes, but to contact other people we're more likely to speak on the phone, send a text, and use email and the Internet.

In all these cases, what passes between you and the other person is information: you're sharing knowledge. The information leaves one person's brain and goes into the other person's.

We only tend to use the word 'data' for information that is in transit between people, in storage in a digital format or where the channel is electric or electromagnetic (like light, radio or infra-red).

	System	Pros	Cons
	Face-to-face	+ can read body language + personal	– not computer-readable – no permanent (hard) copy – costly if people have to travel to meet – open to error (misunderstanding)
	Phone	+ fairly personal + cheap (very cheap if through the Internet)	– not computer-readable – no permanent (hard) copy – open to error (misunderstanding)
	Videophone (3G)	+ fairly personal	– poor image quality – very costly – most people don't have access to it or can't use it
	Text (from a standard mobile phone)	+ people like sending texts + quick	– costly – not often computer-readable – open to error (misunderstanding)
	Hand over a written document or photocopy	+ personal + permanent copy	– not easily computer-readable – no record of exchange
	Fax	+ quick + permanent copy	– not everyone can use it or has access to it
	Post	+ permanent copy	– slow – quite costly – not easily computer-readable
	Email	+ computer-readable + quick + cheap	– some people can't use it or don't have access to it
	Upload to website	+ computer-readable + quick + cheap	– some people can't use it or don't have access to it

Data Transfer Speeds

We measure data transfer rates in bits per second (b/s). The data transfer rate through the normal phone network is about 56 kb/s (56 000 b/s). It's much slower using the normal mobile network, but six times faster with 3G. Transfer rates are even higher with broadband (2 or 3 Mb/s).

Phone Networks

A worldwide system, the normal phone network links a thousand million landlines, usually by wire, or sometimes by micro-waves or radio waves (e.g. in remote places or when using satellites). The mobile (cellphone) network links into this and uses radio waves between the base stations (one per cell) and the handsets.

ISDN (Integrated Services Digital Network) is a fast-access phone network which links two landlines to one computer; it's costly but it was the fastest method until broadband. It is still used as a back-up or instead of broadband. **Broadband** is when data transfers take place at the same time through several channels in the same wires (or cable); this results in higher data transfer rates.

Data & Information Transfer

These two pages cover...

- data compression in the context of communication
- security in the context of communication
- communications systems for messages, conferences, fax and mobile phones

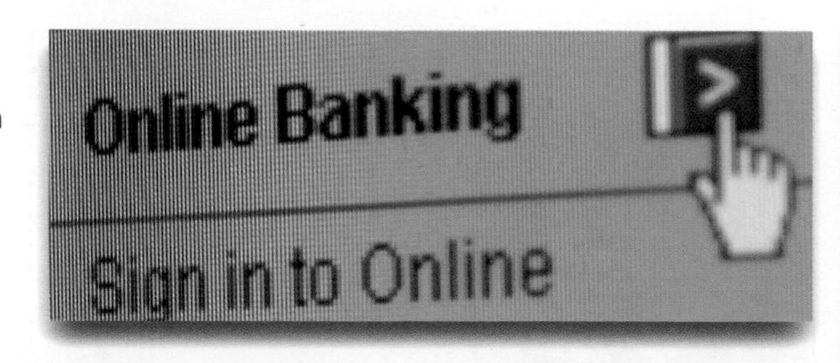

Changing Data in Transit

Squashing or **compressing** data so it takes up less space in store or in transfer has been common for a long time. It's quite easy for software to compress and decompress data when needed. Software can compress any kind of data – like text, speech, photos and moving video – often reducing the space it takes up by 90%. So a 1 MB photo could compress to 100 kB, cutting the transfer time on a 1 Mb/s channel from about eight seconds to less than one second. A **zip file** is one of the most popular compression formats for a PC.

A lot of data is required to create image and sound files, so these files are often compressed. The most common compression formats are as follows:

- **JPEG (Joint Photographic Expert Group)** allows digital photographic images to be compressed to up to 10% of their original size. It doesn't work as well on line-drawing or cartoon images and cannot compress black and white images.
- **GIF (Graphics Interchange Format)** works well with images containing large blocks of colour (e.g. line drawings, black and white images and cartoon images).
- **MPEG (Moving Picture Experts Group)** is the most common format for viewing video images over the Internet. There are different versions of the MPEG format each with a specific use:
  - MPEG-1 for CD-ROM
  - MPEG-2 & 3 for broadcast-quality video
  - MPEG-4 for low bandwidth and Internet use
- **MP3 (MPEG-1 audio layer 3)** allows audio files to be compressed to up to 8% of their size.

It's also common for people to want security for data transfers (and for data in store). The process of 'scrambling' data is called **data encryption** (coding). Software encodes data, for example, when you do on-line banking (e.g. logging on and telling the bank to transfer money to another account). Some people encrypt emails and attachments. Special encryption software and passwords (keys) are required to decode encrypted data.

The most common data change in transfer is between digital and analogue and vice versa. For example, when you send an email from your computer (digital) through the phone system (analogue) or receive one through the analogue phone line to your digital computer. You need a **modem** between the computer and the phone line to convert your computer's outbound digital signals to analogue, and the inbound analogue signals to digital. (You don't need modems with ISDN as it uses digital phone lines.)

Communication Technology

SMS Messages

SMS (short messaging service) messages are like simple emails. They include...
- the text messages you can send and receive on mobile phones and on some computers
- the text-only instant chat messages you can send and receive with some computer email systems.

A chat room is a sort of computer conference where you can chat with more than one person at once.

Conference

Conferences let you share information with more than one person at once:
- by phone: a phone / audio conference – hard to control
- by video (by ISDN or Internet): a video conference – people can see each other as well as hear each other
- by computer (bulletin boards, blogs (see page 84) and wikis (see page 93): like email to groups but the messages stay in store for all to see (text only plus attachments).

  They are hard to control, but you don't all need to be on-line at the same time.

Fax

A fax machine is like a photocopier, but the copy comes out elsewhere (e.g. in an office in another city), having passed through the phone system.

Mobile Phones

Your mobile phone lets you send and receive voice calls and texts if in range of a base station. There's a base station for each cell (area with network coverage). A base station knows which mobiles are in its cell. It transfers a mobile's outward and inward calls and texts by radio waves. The world standard is GSM (Global System for Mobile communication). GPRS (General Packet Radio Services) and 3G (third generation) mobiles cost more but have extra features such as long texts and photo messaging.

These two pages cover...

- the Internet and worldwide web
- Internet Service Providers (ISPs)
- the pros and cons of the Internet
- websites and web pages
- web browsers and search engines
- email, e-commerce and on-line booking

Connecting to the Internet

Your computer can work on its own (stand-alone), or be connected to a local network or the Internet. The Internet is a wide-area network (on a global scale). Some computers are permanently connected to the Internet, especially main servers.

Information can be transmitted through the Internet in a number of ways, the most common being via email and the worldwide web.

The web is an information-sharing facility, consisting of websites made up of text, images, video, sound etc.

ISPs

The main link between a computer and the Internet is an ISP (Internet Service Provider e.g. AOL, Zen), a company that lets you connect your computer to their network which, in turn, is connected to the Internet.

ISPs can provide you with email addresses and act as web hosts, leasing you space to put your web files on their server. Some provide news groups or bulletin boards where articles and messages can be posted for public access.

Every computer that connects to the Internet has its own unique number for logging on. Your ISP can use this number to track your activity on the web.

It will have technology in place to limit your access to the Internet and restrict the amount of information you download depending on the package you have bought.

ISPs can offer different methods of connection: dial-up (using a modem and phone line), broadband, cable or wireless. Low cost connections are good if you only want occasional Internet access but they can be slow and unreliable.

With broadband, data transfers into your computer (downstream) at a faster rate than it transfers the other way (upstream).

The Internet

Pros

- \+ The Internet holds more information than the world's largest library.
- \+ It's easier to get information from the Internet than from a library – if you have access.
- \+ Email access to the whole world is cheap and easy.
- \+ Information can be fully up-to-date (share prices etc.).
- \+ The Internet is highly reliable as you can connect to it at any time.
- \+ The Internet is accessible from any modern computer.

Cons

- – It's hard to find exactly what you want. You may get links to millions of possible websites in response to a search.
- – It's costly to get on-line: the hardware, software and ISP subscriptions aren't cheap.
- – Some people abuse the Internet: you can receive unwanted adverts, spam or viruses.
- – Some people spy on data transfers and steal data (e.g. financial information). We've mentioned the solution, encryption, already (see page 20).
- – You can't trust all the information you find - it may be inaccurate or biased.

Websites and Web Pages

A website is like a house or flat: no other site in the world has the same address. If you enter that address into your browser, you reach the site's **homepage**. After that you can move to the various web pages in the site.

Browsing the Web

A browser (e.g. Internet Explorer and Firefox) lets you...
- access a website if you type in the address (e.g. www.lonsdale-educational.co.uk)
- access a website by linking with a **search engine** like Google, which suggests addresses for the key word(s) you enter (e.g. 'revision'), and allows searches using the logical operators.
- surf the Internet by jumping from site to site using **hyperlinks** (shown by the cursor arrow changing to a hand) and using the 'Back' and 'Forward' options.
- bookmark sites by adding them to your favourites list
- type the first few characters so that it completes the address from your history
- choose your favourite page as your homepage
- download information you need to your computer (but don't forget copyright laws!).

Email

An email can pass between any computers linked to the Internet. It may vary from a few words to millions of MB, maybe with sounds and / or still or video pictures in it or attached to it. When you get an email you can print it, store it, forward it to someone else and / or reply to it. You can also add attachments of documents / files etc. It's easy to send copies of emails to many people at once, perhaps in a group or by using the Cc (carbon copy) or Bcc (blind carbon copy) features. Email is cheap and quick, regardless of distance.

E-commerce

E-commerce is trading through the Internet. It requires a secure facility for transfer of money, and trust. People use the Internet to buy from retailers (books, flowers, software etc.) and from each other (e.g. using auction sites). In the same way, e-banking allows you to check bank accounts, move money by secure data transfer and pay bills on the Internet.

On-line Booking

On-line booking is a kind of e-commerce. You can browse through prices, availability and reviews of different products, then make your booking and arrange payment. You'll often receive the receipt, even the 'tickets', by email within seconds.

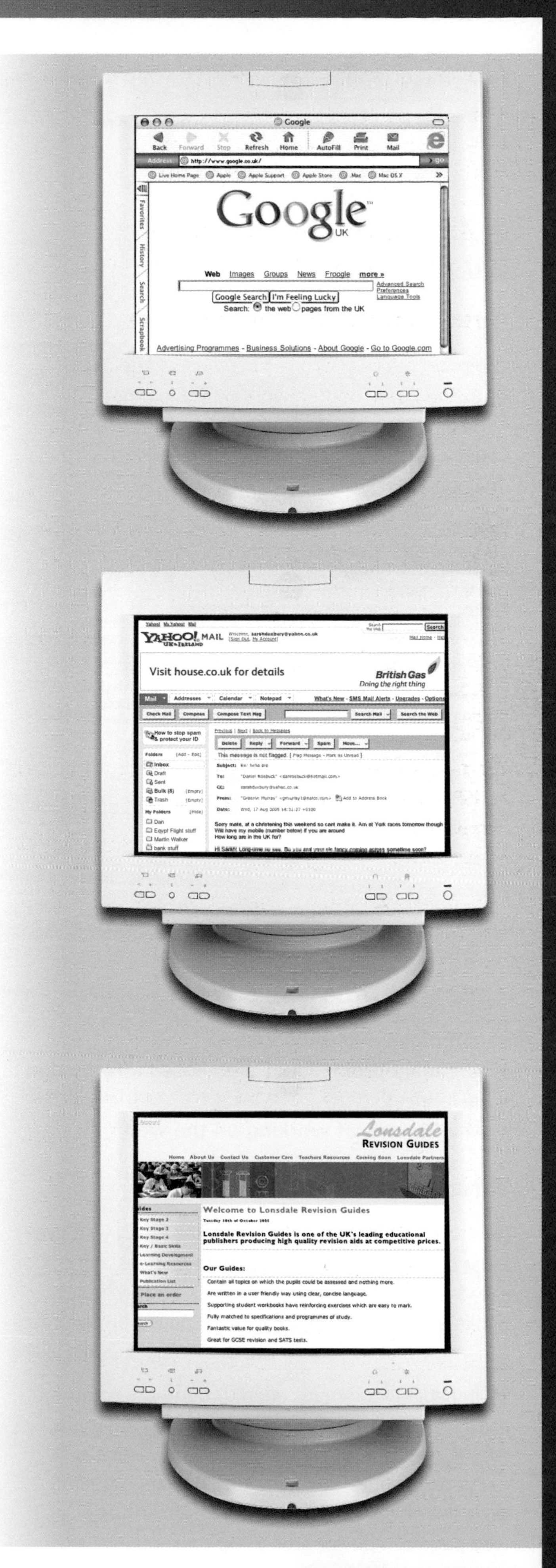

www.dulux.co.uk homepage

The links (circled in the screen shots above) open pages that take you through a guided multimedia tour of how to use the 'Paint a room' feature (right), on the Dulux website

1 Multimedia Pop-up

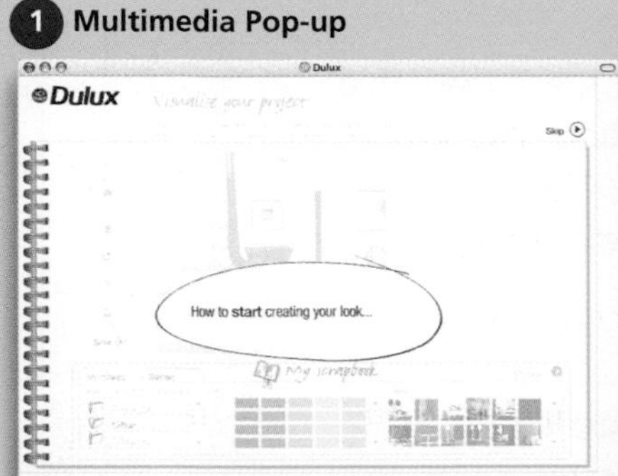

2

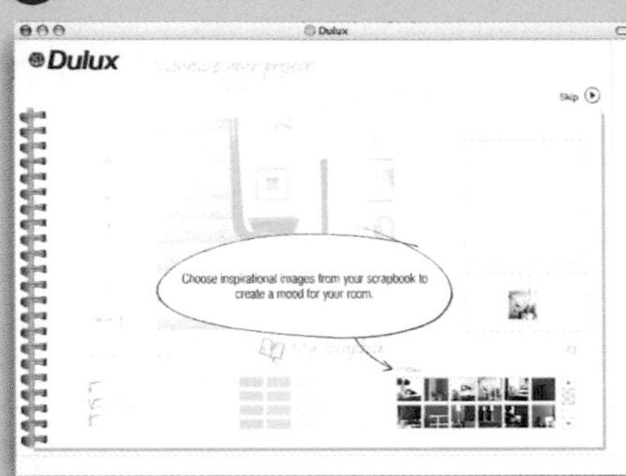

3

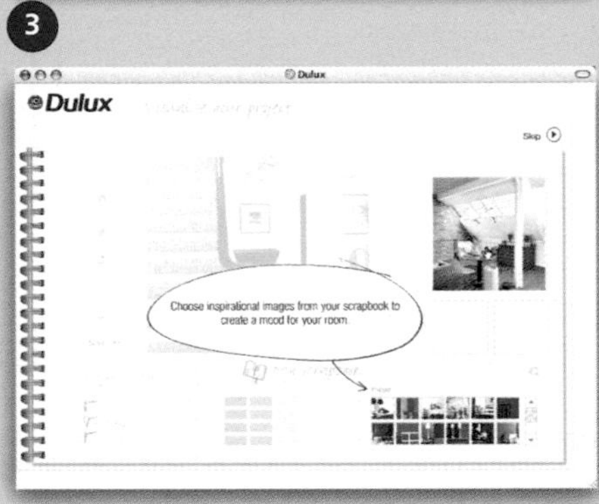

4

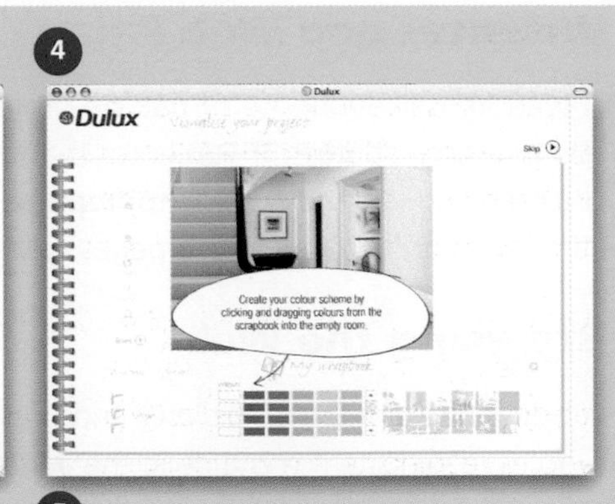

5

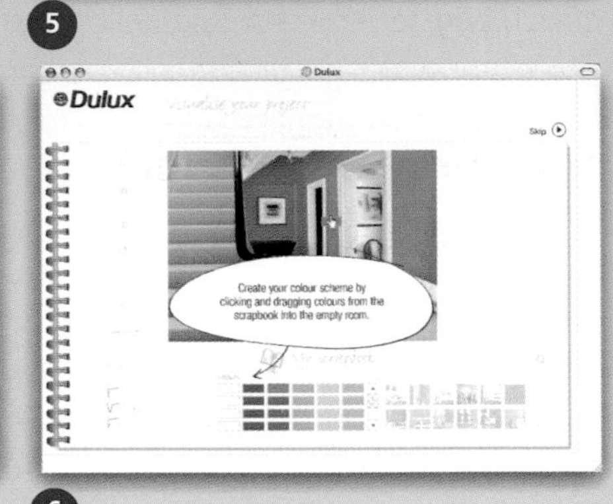

6

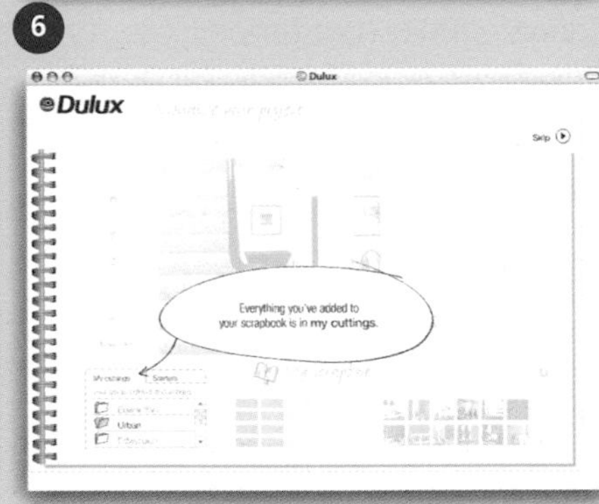

These two pages cover...

- **multimedia and the web**
- **the main problems of web-based information**
- **e-services**
- **the hazards of working on the web**

What is multimedia?

Flick through any book. Which pages catch your eye? Most people prefer the pages with pictures and colour; they least like those with only black and white text. Books use the medium of print on paper, but a screen can incorporate other aspects such as sound and video.

Multimedia is communication through the combined use of text, colour, photos, video, sound and other special effects (as on many web pages). Done well, multimedia pages can communicate very efficiently. With the effects badly done, however, a multimedia web page can be confusing and unhelpful. When designing a web page – or any document – don't overdo these media. The document should always match its purpose and audience.

Can information be bad?

The Internet is a huge source of information, but can you get the information you want? And can you trust the information you get?

When searching, be as specific as you can to narrow down the results e.g. search for 'Iron Bridge Telford' not just 'bridge'. When you get the results, check through the first few to see whether the information is what you want before using it or copying it to your computer. The fact that the Internet has so much information can be a problem so you need to be selective. Searches may lead to undesirable sites (though education networks block these), information may be out of date (you can search by age, but it's not easy) or it may be biased, and sometimes you just can't find what you want.

Internet Advertising

Some firms spend huge sums sending out junk mail – they believe it's worth the cost (paper and postage). But sending spam emails is much cheaper. It's against the law but the fines are tiny, so it's very tempting.

Other forms of Internet advertising are legal, but they can be a problem if they interfere with what you want to do. For example, 'pop-ups' can cover up what you're reading which is a nuisance, and sometimes a search engine returns results that are adverts rather than information sources.

Internet Group Work

There are various ways computers facilitate group work.

- Email to groups. Your email address book can include groups (such as school friends and relatives). It's just as easy to send an email to a group as to one person. If you receive a group email, you can reply to all in one go (unless it's an email newsletter, which is one way only), or just to the sender.
- The computer conference (or bulletin board, or news group) is like sending email to a group but all the messages appear in clearer lists on members' screens.
- In a chat room you can send a message to everyone else there at that time and see everyone's messages. Of course chat rooms do have dangers as you never really know who you're chatting to.

E-services

We've already mentioned e-banking and on-line booking; these are e-services, things you can get on-line that aren't physical products. Other examples are:

- travel planners – for plotting a car / lorry / public transport route around the country
- enquiry centres and on-line information desks – e.g. for tourists, parents and prospective students
- customer support – to get help for something that's not working as it should
- insurance sites – to get a quote on-line and then buy the policy (e.g. for cars, travel, house contents)
- consumer advice – information about products from different companies (e.g. gas supply, cars and vacuum cleaners) so you can compare prices, features etc.

Pop-ups can cover up a web page when you're trying to look at it.

Internet Hazard	Solution / Protection
Virus: a malicious program that spreads by inserting copies of itself into other programs / documents.	**Virus checker software** alerts the user to the presence of a virus and helps remove it.
Worm: a malicious program that can copy itself to other computers / networks.	
Trojan (horse): a malicious program disguised as useful software (e.g. a game, applications).	
Hacker: someone who tries to access your machine to steal data or use it illegally (e.g. to make an attack on a major site).	**Firewall software** blocks unauthorised transfers to / from the Internet.
Spam: junk email or chat messages, often advertising something.	**Spam killer software** prevents these downloading.
Spyware: a kind of virus that reports what you do and information about you.	**Spyware killer software** checks for and removes spyware.

Knowing the System

These four pages cover...

- the three types of software
- software utilities
- user interfaces
- how operating system software and the CPU work together
- the parts of the CPU
- multi-systems

Application software

There are three types of software:

1. **Operating system software:** the integral type of software. This software works automatically to operate the information system.
2. **Application software:** the programs the user works with, for example, word processing and spreadsheet programs.
3. **Program language software:** enables the user to create application software. Program languages include Logo and BASIC.

The hardware needs operating system software to operate it. The user needs application software to achieve what he / she wants from the information system.

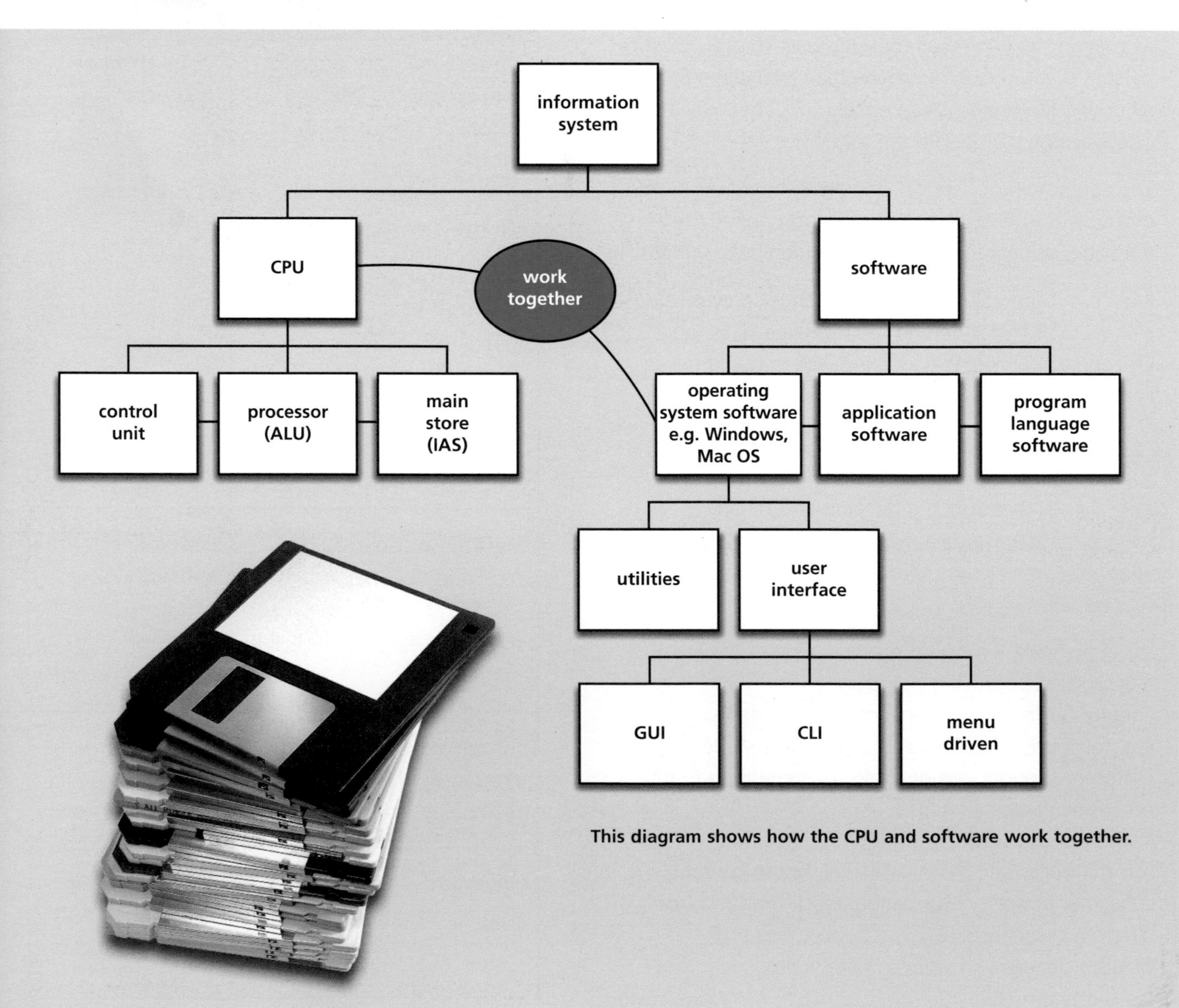

This diagram shows how the CPU and software work together.

Operating system software is a form of data that instructs information systems - the information system is useless without it. Operating system software is not the same for all information systems (because their CPUs are not the same).

The operating system software of PCs (Windows) differs from that used in Apple machines (Mac OS). There are new versions of Windows and Mac OS software every few years, which means older machines generally have older operating system software with fewer features.

Operating system software must try to cover all needs but older versions don't work well with newer technology such as DVD data storage and digital cameras.

Little bits of operating system software called device drivers try to cover all peripheral handling needs.

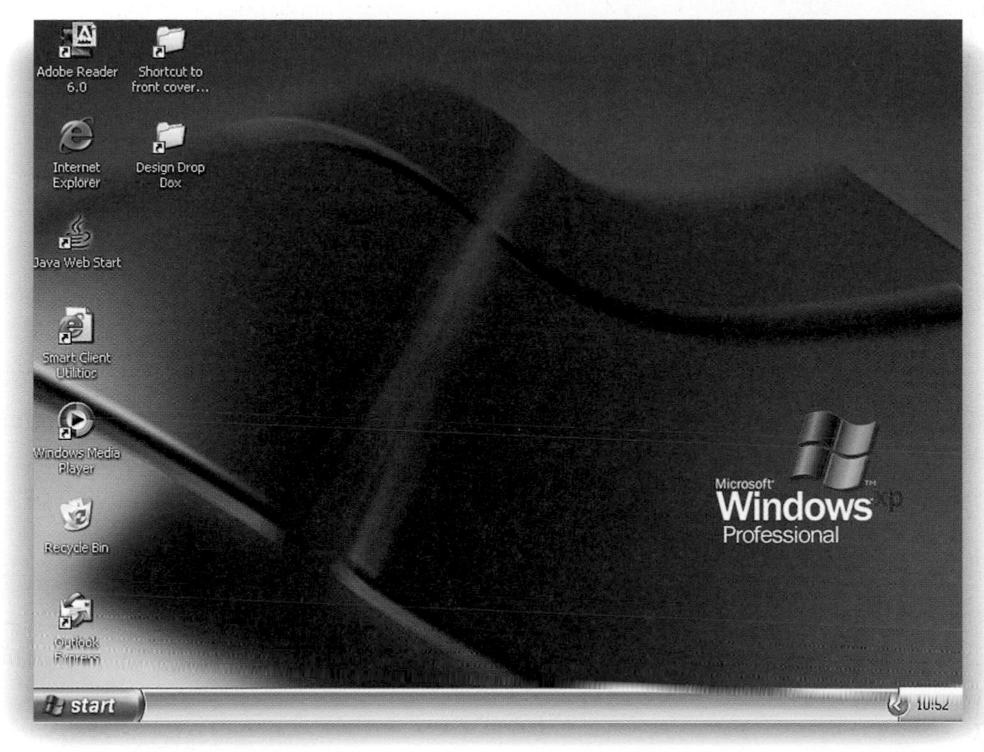

Operating system software

Utilities

Operating system software contains small programs known as utilities which perform specific tasks. For example...

- **log-on:** to manage the user name and password at start-up
- **back-up:** to ensure the backing store keeps a copy of a file's old version when you save the latest version
- **file deletion:** to ensure the backing store gets rid of the record of a file when you ask to delete it
- **reset:** to try to rescue things if you have a problem and press CTRL+ALT+DEL
- **screen blanking:** to clear the screen or start the screen saver when you're not working at the computer
- **error handling:** to send you the right error message (e.g. if the printer's yellow ink runs out).

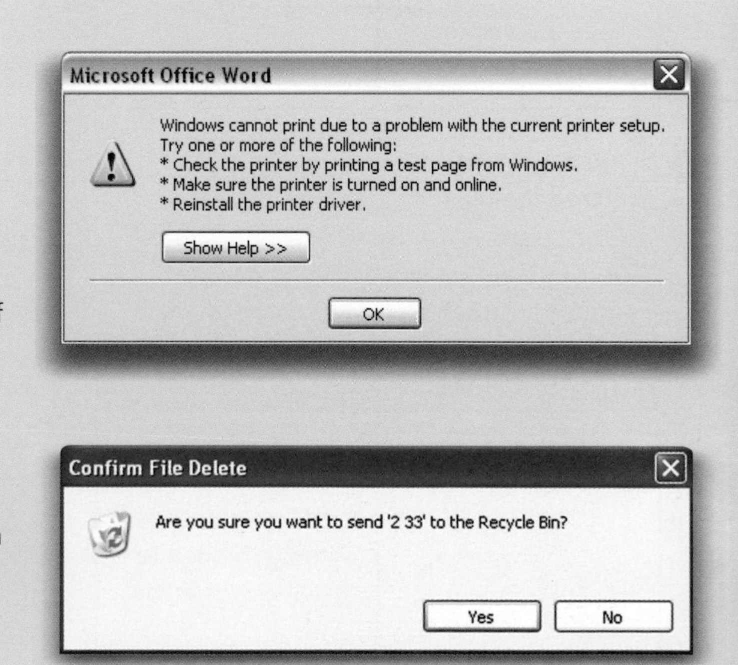

User Interfaces

A user interface is the link between an information system and the user; it is part of the operating system software. There are three types of user interface:

1. **Graphical user interface (GUI)**
Most computers use a GUI. GUIs use icons, images and menus and are controlled by a cursor (mouse). An example is Microsoft Windows.

Pros	Cons
+ easy to use + looks appealing + less operational errors are made as it's so easy to use	– takes up a lot of disk space – takes up a lot of RAM (for graphics) – can slow the computer down

2. **Command line (or command driven) interface (CLI)**
CLIs use only textual input; a prompt appears on screen and the user then types in the command. An example of a CLI is MSDOS.

Pros	Cons
+ uses little memory + uses little processing power + can be quick to operate once you know how	– difficult to use

3. **Menu driven interface**
As the name suggests, the menu driven interface displays menus on screen for the user. Each menu has sub-menus. Menu driven interfaces are often found on mobile phones.

Pros	Cons
+ easy to use	– can take a long time – there may be lots of menus to go through to get to where you want

Operating System Software and the CPU Working Together

Information system hardware requires software to operate it. The core of any information system is the CPU. The data processed here includes instructions from the operating system software; this data is in a simple program language (patterns of 0s and 1s). Operating system software instructions control everything the CPU does.

There are three parts to the CPU, each controlled by instructions from operating system software:

1. **Control unit**
This co-ordinates the whole system. It controls the data flow within the CPU and the data input and output (i.e. to and from the peripherals), and monitors the actions of the peripherals to ensure commands are carried out correctly.

2. **Processor (Arithmetic and logical unit, ALU)**
This processes the data. It makes calculations (e.g. 5 x 9) and logical comparisons (e.g. 21 is less than 23).

3. **Main store (Immediate Access Store, IAS)**
This is the CPU's inbuilt memory. The CPU reads data from backing storage (e.g. floppy disks) and temporarily stores it in the main store (RAM or ROM). It is quicker to access data from the main store than from other locations.

Example of a graphical user interface

Multi-systems

The operating system software of a simple information system, such as a GSM mobile phone, is very basic.

The more complex a system is, the more the operating system software has to do – so the more complex the software must be. A mainframe computer has much more complex operating system software than a desktop computer. The main reason for this is that a mainframe needs more power than a desktop because…

- it's a **multi-user** system: thousands of people may use it at the same time (e.g. a large firm or university), each with his / her own workstation (terminal)
- it's a **multi-processor** system: it has to control perhaps thousands of processors working in parallel (as when number-crunching, e.g. code-breaking)
- it's a **multi-tasking** system: groups of processors work on more than one task (e.g. number-crunching, running a video conference and mail-merge printing) at the same time.

But even a desktop with multimedia needs complex operating system software, as does a network of two stations.

Even small networks (e.g. in school) need one machine working full time as a server, which controls the others, and the system as a whole.

The Word Processing Family

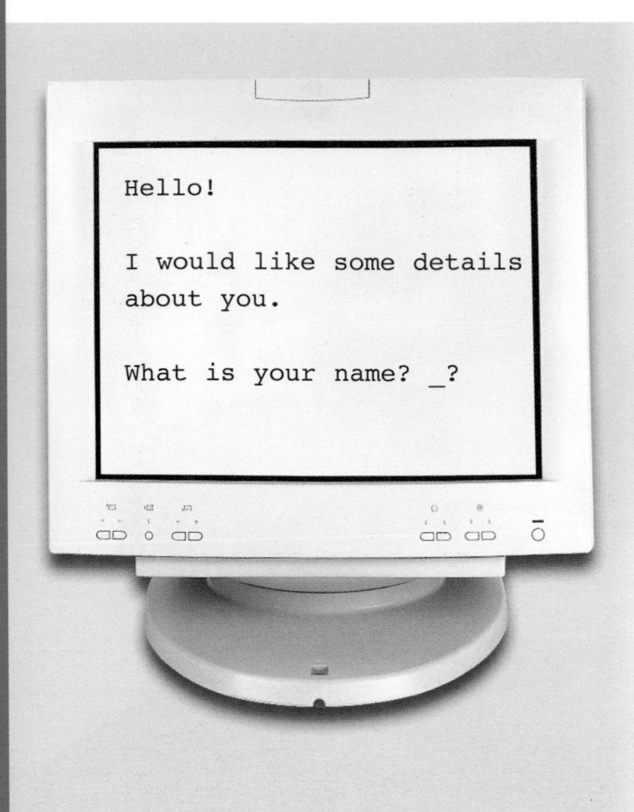


```
>10 PRINT "Hello!"
>20 PRINT
>30 PRINT "I would like
some details about you."
>40 PRINT
>50 INPUT "What is your
name?", NAME$
...
>run
Hello!

I would like some details
about you.

What is your name? _?
```

BASIC program language

These four pages cover...

- **application software programs**
- **word processor programs**
- **personal / desktop publisher programs**
- **presentation software programs**
- **web page design programs**

Application Programs

The purpose of any application software program is to meet users' needs. Without operating system software, computer hardware won't work at all; without application software, it can't do what you want it to. Sometimes people have application software specially made for them, for example, if they have a particular, unusual need. In the past programmers designed legal software, hotel booking programs and learning software to meet clients' needs in small markets. These programs slowly became standard applications as information technology developed and became more commonly used.

A program language program is needed to write an application program. The screen shot alongside shows an example of the BASIC program language. Instructions starting with a number are part of the program and `run` is the command to carry out the instructions.

You can set up an application program to match your needs, such as screen layout and what goes on the menus and toolbars.

Some applications are only available for certain systems; in other cases there are versions for the different systems (like Windows, UNIX, Mac OS).

Some applications are in **suites** (groups of programs) which allow easy transfer of data between their programs, as with MS Works, MS Office and OpenOffice. Suites like these usually consist of at least a word processor and a spreadsheet.

The most frequently used application program is the word processor (e.g. MS Word or WordPerfect).

Word processing produces mainly text documents that are…
- fit for the audience you're aiming at
- fit for the purpose (passing on certain information)
- easy to design and produce.

Other application programs which have a similar purpose are…
- personal / desktop publishers
- presentation programs (e.g. MS PowerPoint)
- web page design software (e.g. Macromedia Dreamweaver).

Word Processing Features

Page Layout
- Page orientation: portrait is usually used for text documents but (like our samples alongside) landscape can be better for a notice or a slide.
- The sizes of the top, bottom, left and right margins can be altered (the top and bottom margins can hold headers or footers of almost any size).
- The space between paragraphs and columns can be altered to fit more / less text on the page.

Text Layout
- Columns can be used to make the text easier to read.
- Indenting lines or using tabulation (tabs) changes the look of a paragraph, for example to emphasise a point, and affects how easy it is to read.
- Lists and tables (maybe with numbers / letters / bullet points) can present data more clearly.

Graphics
- Page borders (with different styles / shading) can make a page stand out.
- Features like arrows and bubbles can add to a page's impact and value.
- Inserting a picture (line drawing, photo etc.) attracts readers, but it must be relevant and useful.

Spelling and Grammar
- Spell check.
- Grammar check.
- Thesaurus.

Compare the two documents on the right. Do you agree that the document at the bottom is better for reader and purpose?

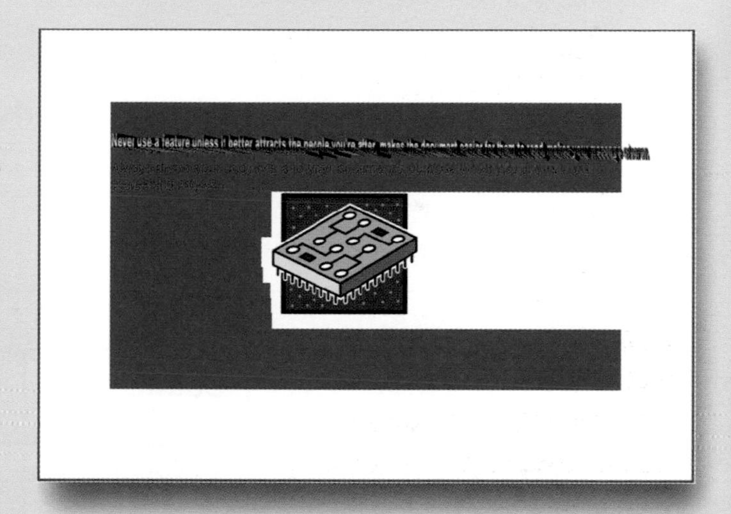

Word Processing - dos and don'ts!

Never...

use a feature unless it
- better attracts the people you're aiming at
- makes the document easier for them to read
- makes your message clearer.

Always...

define your audience and your document's purpose when you plan a word processing project.

Good and bad examples of the use of word processing features.

The Word Processing Family

Presenting Text and Graphics

- **Word processor:** This is generally used for straightforward documents: letters, memos, essays, posters, invitations etc. It offers text, graphics and special effects. You can also **mail merge** documents (see page 50).
- **Desktop publisher:** The personal or desktop publisher allows the user to add a professional high-quality finish to documents. It is normally used where more control is required over the positioning of text and graphics. Most publisher programs offer **frames** (boxes for holding any data, e.g. text, pictures).
- **Presentation program:** This can process text but is specifically used for displaying information on a screen or using a projector. It is normally used for small amounts of text, e.g. to illustrate key points. You can add interactivity, **hot spots** to link you to different screens in the show, and **hyperlinks** to other places. Pages can include video, animation and other aspects of multimedia, like sound. If your audience has the opportunity to interact, the show is likely to hold their interest and is therefore easier to learn from. (It's the same with paper documents.)
- **Web page design program:** Such a package is also for documents seen on screen, like the pages you get when you use the Internet to look at a site. They can be interactive, contain multimedia, hot spots, hyperlinks and imported text and pictures. This software differs from the rest because you create documents using a special program language called HTML. So each page is in fact a program, a set of instructions to tell the system what to do.

Features of the Word Processing Family

Make sure you know these techniques and how and when to use them. Look at the sample documents opposite to see how these features can be used.

Feature		Examples			Comment
Font	**type**	Arial	Comic	Brush Script	Ensure font is easy for planned audience to read.
	size	8 point	12 point	18 point	Ensure size matches the document's purpose.
	style	**bold**	*italic*	underlined	Avoid underlining in most documents.
	colour	black	red	yellow	Keep colours clear, and don't forget colour-blind readers (almost 10% of males).
	highlight	white / none	red	yellow	
Alignment		left / right	centred	justified	Stick to left except in some lists and notices.
List type		none at all	❍ bullet ❍ like ❍ this	3.2 - numbers (b) - or letters Q3 - or like this	Bulleting and numbering are great for lists. Choose style aspects that best match purpose, and stick to them.
Borders and shading					You can apply borders and shading to anything.
Inserted graphics		clipart	shapes	photos	You can insert sound (audio) files and movies (animations and video) into e-documents; look at the 'Insert' menu for other things you can drop into your text document.

Fonts

Different font styles, colours and sizes should only be used if they add to the appeal of a document and make its purpose more clear.

Large font size, upper case, bold and colour are used in example a) to draw attention to the important points. Altering line spacing and centrally aligning the text also suit the purpose of this document (i.e. a poster).

STOP THE AIRPORT NOW!

There will be a public meeting to discuss our objections to the proposals to build a new runway at Clapthorpe Airfield.

Register your protest NOW!

Join us at the Village Hall

7.45 pm on Wednesday 3rd June

Meet your local councillors and hear what they have to say.

DON'T DELAY PROTEST TODAY

a) Good

STOP THE AIRPORT NOW!

There will be a public meeting to discuss our objections to the proposals to build a new runway at

Clapthorpe Airfield.

Register your protest NOW!

Join us at the Village Hall

7.45 pm on

Wednesday 3rd June

Meet your local councillors and hear what they have to say.

DON'T

DELAY PROTEST TODAY

b) Bad

Bullets and Numbers

Bullets and numbers can be used to help present information more clearly. They should be used consistently and must not vary in size or alignment.

Numbers are used in example a) to present a list of tasks in order of how they should be done. This makes the important points within the document stand out.

John,

Thanks for stepping in while I'm away. There are a number of things that need to be done before you leave tonight:

1. Set the message on the answering machine
2. Check that the photocopier and all the computers have been turned off
3. Set the security alarm & lock up
4. Drop the keys off at Rachael's

Have a great time this weekend, I'll see you on Monday.

Kathy

a) Good

Sarah,

There are a number of things that you need to think about before next week's meeting. These include:

- Staffing requirements
- Set-up costs
  - Production costs
- Delivery dates

I look forward to discussing these with you next Tuesday.

Clive

b) Bad

Images

Poor use of images can spoil a document and draw attention away from the main points. Aim for quality rather than quantity and think carefully about the position of each image.

One simple image is enough for the purpose of this document (i.e. a menu) and adds to its appeal. Central alignment, coloured breaks between lines of text and a simple border help to create a clear, attractive document in example a) which is perfectly fit for the purpose and audience.

MENU

Leek and Potato Soup

-o-0-o-

Trout in Almonds

-o-0-o-

Braised Lamb Shanks

-o-0-o-

Selection of English Cheeses

-o-0-o-

Coffee and Mints

a) Good

MENU

Leek and Potato Soup

-o-0-o-

Trout in Almonds

-o-0-o-

Braised Lamb Shanks

-o-0-o-

Selection of English Cheeses

-o-0-o-

Coffee and Mints

b) Bad

Graphics & Images

These two pages cover…

- **graphics and images – how to get them into a document**
- **graphics sources**
- **bit-mapping and vector graphics**
- **computer-aided design**

A graphic is any part of a document on paper or on screen that isn't text. The examples below are graphics.

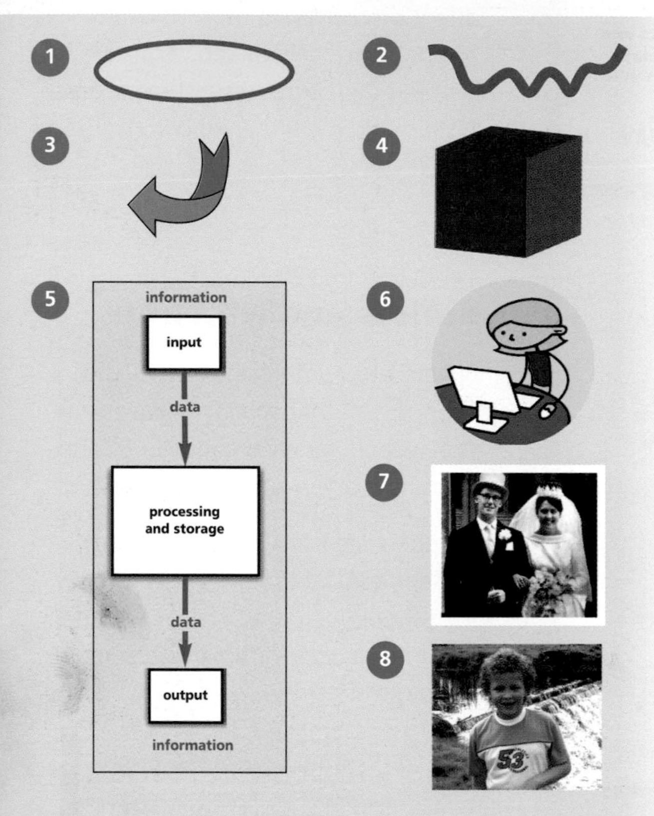

Where do we get graphics from?

- **1** came from a line and shape drawing program in Word.
- **2** came from a freehand drawing program, also part of Word.
- **3** was copied and pasted from page 32.
- **4** is from another graphics system, again part of Word.
- **5** We scanned the diagram (on page 6) but we could have used a special drawing program.
- **6** is from a clipart collection in Word.
- **7** was a photo scanned into the computer, then cropped.
- **8** The input unit for this photo was a digital camera. Link the camera to the computer, run the data transfer utility and the photo is saved and appears on screen.

So, we can get graphics into store in various ways. Try to practise them all, but always make sure your uses are fit for audience and purpose.

Graphics Sources

Graphics library – you can select graphics from a library (within graphics software) and modify them using library software before inserting them into your document.

The Internet / other documents – images can be copied and pasted but beware of copyright laws.

Photos, images and graphics from documents, magazines, flyers etc. – you can scan them into a computer and edit them before inserting them into the document. Again beware of copyright laws.

Photos from a digital camera – images can be loaded into the computer and edited (e.g. cropping, altering the contrast) but make sure you take into account privacy issues.

Other software programs – you can import graphics that have been created in other software programs, for example, a computer-aided design program or Paint, which offers a range of brushes, lines, textures, shapes and effects as well as text entry.

Screen shot – by pressing 'Prt Sc' on your keyboard and then selecting 'paste' in another program you can insert an image of what appears on your computer screen.

It is easy to process a basic shape using graphics library software. Manipulating an arrow graphic can give many different options, as shown below. But what about processing other forms of graphics data like photos?

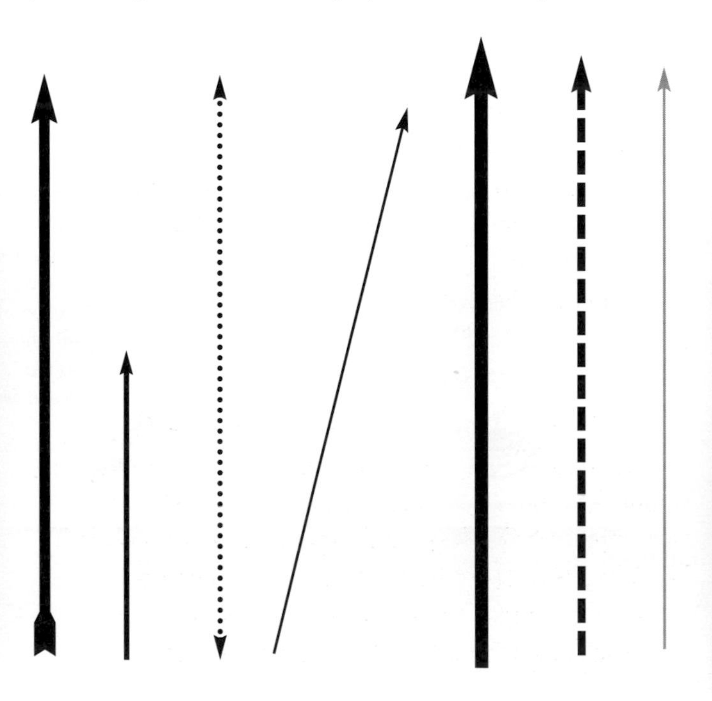

Two Ways to Produce a Line

If you wanted to draw a line between two points on a piece of paper you would use a pencil and ruler. The same method can be used on a computer, with a graphics pad, and is called **bit-mapping** (diagram a). The picture is made up of pixels (tiny dots), and the position and colour of each pixel is stored by the computer. If you zoom into the picture, the pixels become enlarged so the lines on the image are not clear (diagram b). When this happens we say the image looks pixellated. Bit-mapping takes up a lot of storage space (4 bytes per pixel) and is no good for precise drawings.

Vector graphics are better than bit-mapping for producing precise drawings. A line is defined by its end points, and the style and colour of the line between the points (diagram c). If you zoom in, the quality of the line stays the same so the image is still clear (diagram d). You only need a few bytes to store the whole image and it's easy to change one detail, so vector graphics are usually used for high-quality drawings.

a) bit-mapped

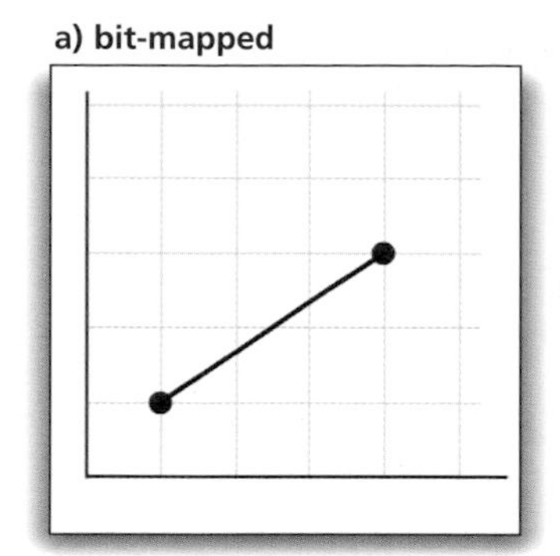

b) bit-mapped zoom

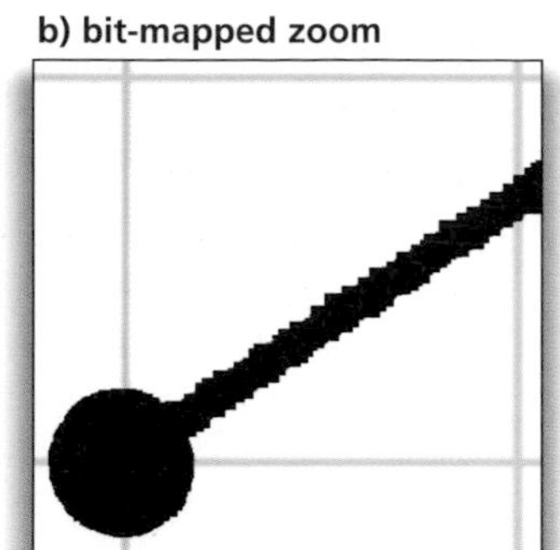

c) Vector graphics

d) Vector graphics zoom

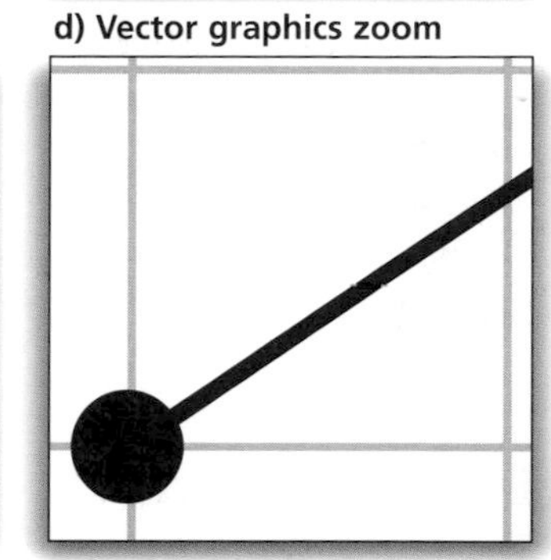

a) original photo.

b) changing brightness and contrast, and cropping.

c) zooming in, changing the smoke to flames and pasting in buildings from another photo.

d) restyling like a modern oil painting.

Manipulating Images

It's easy to change one detail of a vector graphic drawing but not one detail of a bit-mapped image, e.g. a photo. Most things you can do with a bit-mapped image apply to the whole image or to a big chunk of it. The photos above show the changes you can make with graphics software; all changes affect big chunks of the image.

Computer-Aided Design

Computer-aided design (CAD) helps people like architects, engineers and designers to produce precise and accurate drawings. The CAD system stores the details of each aspect of the drawing (circle, shadow, string of words etc.) as a few bytes. It's then very easy to edit each detail. Input tends to be with a graphics pad; users have large screens and plotters to produce hard copy.

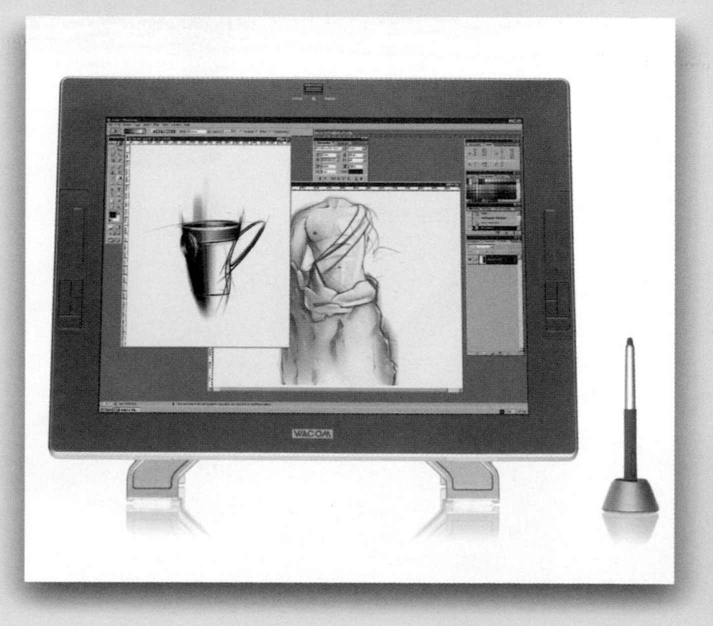

Spreadsheets

These six pages cover...

- **spreadsheets and their uses**
- **rows, columns and cells**
- **formatting spreadsheet cells**
- **spreadsheet formulae**
- **absolute and relative values**
- **spreadsheet graphs and charts**

	A	B	C	D	E
1		B1			
2					
3					
4			C3:D4		
5					
6					
7					
8					
9					
10					
11					
12					
13					

Sheet1 / Sheet2 / Sheet3

After the word processor, the spreadsheet is the most widely used application in the office. A spreadsheet is a grid of cells, set out in vertical lettered columns and horizontal numbered rows. Extra pages (sheets) can be used for extra grids. (See spreadsheet opposite.)

Each cell has an address of column letter + row number, for example `B1`. The address of a block (or range) of cells has the form `C3:D4` (i.e. the 4 cells from `C3` to `D4`). (See spreadsheet opposite.)

Entering Data

There are several ways to get data into spreadsheet cells: you can type it in, load it from a data file (as with data on the Internet), or replicate (copy and paste) it from elsewhere (e.g. a word processed table) or from other cells in the spreadsheet.

What are spreadsheets used for?

- To enter data so it can be processed very quickly (e.g. to find the highest and lowest attendance figures of students at a school or to find the average test score).
- To sort the data (e.g. into alphabetical order) to make it easier to use.
- To search the data (e.g. to find all students with the surname 'Johnson').
- To produce graphs and charts (see page 39).
- To model a situation using formulae. Spreadsheets can be very useful models because input values can be changed in order to find out the effects on the outputs. For example, a shop keeper can find out how his / her takings would vary if the rate of VAT went up from 17.5% to 20%. This is a **'what if...?' model** (see page 42).

Data Types and Cell Formats

A spreadsheet cell can be left empty, or can contain one of the following types of data:

- **Number** (anything with a numerical value). You can use currency or accounts format (if you want the £ sign to appear automatically), percentage formats or various date and time formats. With most formats you can choose how many decimal places to use (e.g. 1.2345 or 1.2). Negative values can be shown with a minus sign or made red to stand out.
- **Text** (any string of keyboard characters). Spreadsheets are number processors, but they can also process text strings to an extent. You can format text in cells by changing font colour, size and style etc.
- **Formula** (works out a value from the values in other cells). A formula (in the case of MS Excel) starts with an equals sign ('='). The formula used to calculate the value of cell D3 in the spreadsheet below is `=360/C3`

	A	B	C	D	E	F
1			Properties			
2	Name	Shape	No. of Sides	Exterior Angle (°)	Interior Angle (°)	
3	Triangle		3	120	60	
4	Square		4	90	90	
5	Pentagon		5	72	108	
6	Hexagon		6	60	120	

- **Graphics** (shapes, pictures, diagrams, photos). You can insert graphics into any cell or range of cells.

  With the right software, sound, documents and presentations can also be stored in cells.

Spreadsheet Formulae

The following are all examples of spreadsheet formulae:

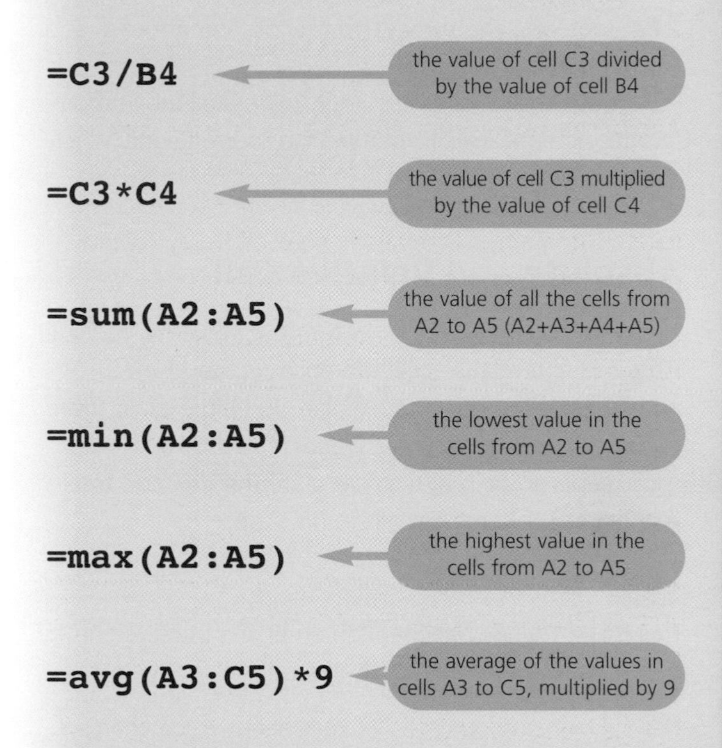
=C3/B4
the value of cell C3 divided by the value of cell B4
=C3*C4
the value of cell C3 multiplied by the value of cell C4
=sum(A2:A5)
the value of all the cells from A2 to A5 (A2+A3+A4+A5)
=min(A2:A5)
the lowest value in the cells from A2 to A5
=max(A2:A5)
the highest value in the cells from A2 to A5
=avg(A3:C5)*9
the average of the values in cells A3 to C5, multiplied by 9

IF Formula

An IF formula checks whether a condition is met and displays one of two options in the cell depending on the result. The format of the formula is:

=IF(condition, action if condition is true, action if condition is false)

For example...

=IF(B3<5,"yes","no")

Look at the spreadsheet below. If the value in cell B3 is lower than 5, 'yes' will be displayed. If the value in cell B3 is not lower than 5, 'no' will be displayed. So, if fewer than 5 pieces of homework have been handed in, the student will get detention (i.e. 'yes').

	A	B	C
1	**Summer term: Number of homework pieces handed in**		
2	Name	Number of homeworks	Detention?
3	Ahmad, S	8	no
4	Burton, E	10	no
5	Hemsley, R	3	yes
6	Smith, L	4	yes

Plan Ahead

When designing a spreadsheet, do just what you would with any other document:

- Be clear who the spreadsheet is for (e.g. a friend) and what it is for (purpose).
- Plan the layout (columns, rows, formulae etc.) before entering data, and format with colour etc. only when it's working.
- Use a small set of input data to test formulae.
- You can change details if and when you need to; you can insert and delete columns and rows, merge cells and edit formulae. Each time you change an item of data, the formulae in the sheet will automatically recalculate to take into account the change made. Make sure you don't delete a cell that is needed for a calculation later on!

Absolute and Relative Cell References

Absolute and relative cell references relate to the addresses of the cells in formulae. To help explain these terms, we will use a spreadsheet created by a shopkeeper to help him to calculate the VAT and total sale prices for items he sells in his shop.

Look at ❶

Cell B4 – The shopkeeper can enter the price of one biro (before VAT is added) in this cell.

Cell C4 – The amount of VAT that needs to be charged for each biro is displayed in this cell. This value is calculated by multiplying the value in cell B4 by the percentage multiplier for 17.5% (0.175) which can be found in cell C1.

Cell D4 – This cell shows the total sale price, which is calculated by adding the values in cells B4 and C4.

The rest of columns C and D can be calculated using the same formulae. So we can copy cells C4 and D4 down into rows 5 to 8 (see ❷). The cell references in the formulae in column D are relative cell references because the cell references in the formulae change depending on the row. So when a formula with relative cell references is copied and pasted, the spreadsheet automatically amends the cell references.

In column C, the first part of the formula is a relative cell reference, but for the second part the same cell reference (cell C1) is used to calculate each value. This is an absolute reference and is entered using dollar signs, e.g. $C$1. Any cell reference with a dollar sign in front of it will remain unchanged when the formula is copied to other cells.

So remember: An absolute cell reference in a formula remains exactly the same wherever it is moved to in the spreadsheet. A relative cell reference changes according to where the formula is pasted to.

❶

	A	B	C	D
1		VAT (at 17.5%) =	0.175	
2				
3	**Item**	**Price before VAT**	**VAT**	**sale price (£)**
4	**Biro**		=B4*$C$1	=C4+B4
5	**4x AA Batteries**			
6	**crisps**			
7	**mountain bike**			
8	**torch**			

❷

	A	B	C	D
1		VAT (at 17.5%) =	0.175	
2				
3	**Item**	**Price before VAT**	**VAT**	**sale price (£)**
4	**Biro**		=B4*$C$1	=C4+B4
5	**4x AA Batteries**		=B5*$C$1	=C5+B5
6	**crisps**		=B6*$C$1	=C6+B6
7	**mountain bike**		=B7*$C$1	=C7+B7
8	**torch**		=B8*$C$1	=C8+B8

Graphs and Charts

Spreadsheets can also be used to plot a graph or chart (e.g. heights of pupils or results of a science exam). To produce a graph, highlight the relevant data and choose the type of chart / graph you want from the toolbar.

You can produce bar graphs, line graphs, pie charts and scatter graphs, label the axes and key, and give them headings. A spreadsheet can produce graphs instantly and accurately.

The graphs at the bottom of the page were produced from the spreadsheet below.

Phillpots East Midlands Sales.xls

	A	B	C	D	E	F
1						
2	**East Midlands Sales Team**					
3						
4	**Sales Person**	**April**	**May**	**June**	**July**	**Total**
5	J. Sunil	£38,650	£36,275	£35,120	£32,015	£142,060
6	R. Simpson	£29,390	£34,180	£31,455	£30,250	£125,275
7	D. Sands	£31,000	£32,550	£33,500	£34,955	£132,005
8						
9	**Monthly Minimum**	£29,390	£32,550	£31,455	£30,250	

1 Bar graph / chart

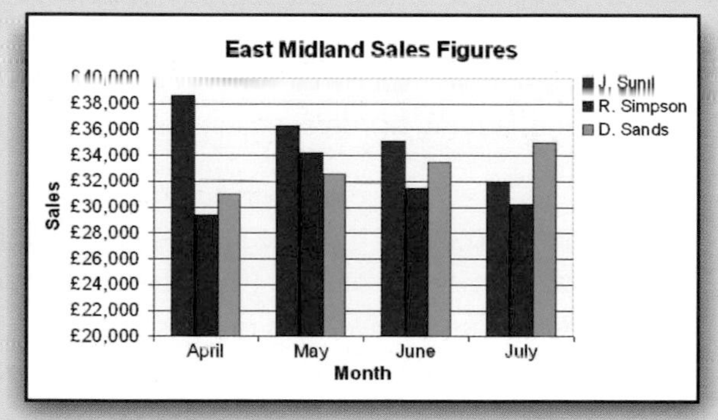

2 Pie chart

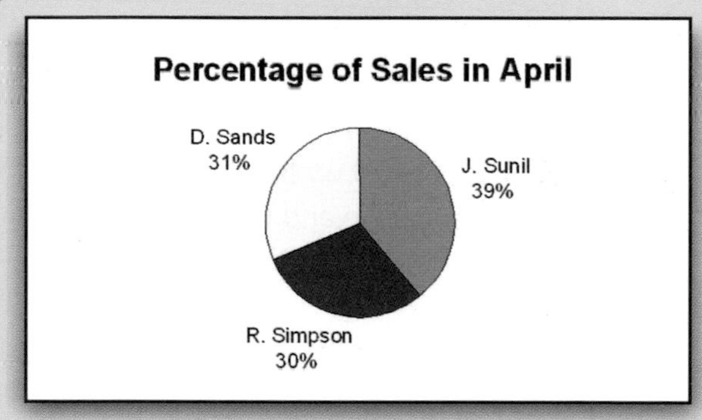

3 Line graph

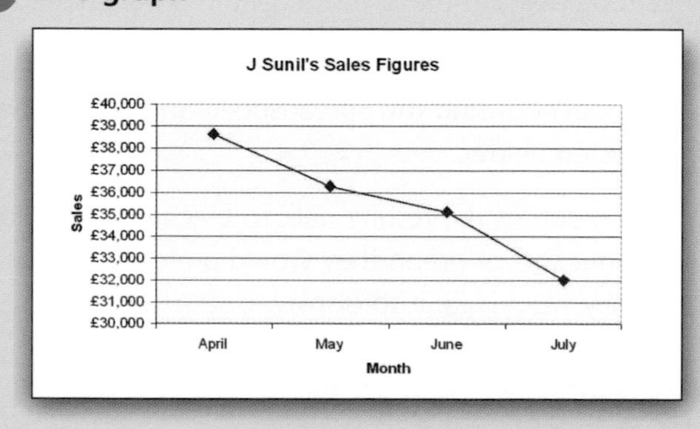

4 Scatter graph

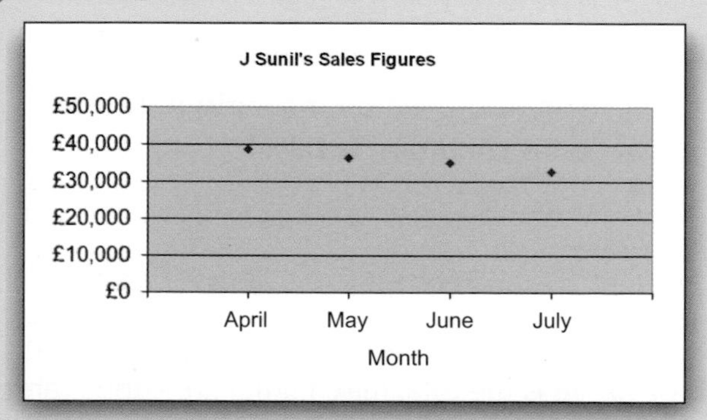

Be careful with scatter graphs on spreadsheets – they don't always work very well. It's usually better to use one of the other types.

Spreadsheet Development

These two pages show how to develop a GCSE-level spreadsheet solution to a problem.

The problem: A school teacher wants to store pupils' marks for pieces of work completed over the course of a year to help her to predict their GCSE grade bands.

We know the first things to consider are the purpose and likely user of the spreadsheet, so now we can proceed straight to developing a simple system.

(Note: a coursework project involves much more than just the development stage – see pages 54-65).

The numbered examples on the opposite page correspond to the following numbered paragraphs.

1. This is an initial design for the spreadsheet. When designing it you must consider data input, processing and data output. The data will come from the teacher's paper mark book.

2. Once it's ready to use, you can insert a number of columns for marks for each section of the course, with the date and total for each column (homework, etc.). The teacher may, at a later stage, choose to hide columns that are not needed all the time.

   It is at this stage that formulae are entered. The formulae in row 6 (E6 and I6) show the total marks available for those parts of the course. The formulae in row 8 (E8 and I8) add up the student's marks for those parts of the course and it is these formulae that will be replicated for each student. These formulae work even if you later add, hide or take away columns. The formulae in column J calculate each student's overall total; you'll need to edit them as you add new parts of the course. The =IF formula in K8 is an extension-level concept (see page 37). It is explained below:

   =IF(condition, action if condition is true, action if condition is false)

   So by applying this to our spreadsheet we get:

   e.g. **=IF(J8/$J$6>0.5,"Pass","Fail")**

   This means 'divide each student's mark in column J by J6'. J6 is the total maximum mark – this is an absolute cell reference, shown by $J$6, which means it is a constant in each formula. If the answer is greater than 0.5 (50%), "Pass" is displayed in the relevant cell in column K. If the answer is less than or equal to 0.5 (50%), "Fail" is displayed.

3. We must then check that the spreadsheet works by entering some sample data (e.g. marks for one piece of work from three students) and making sure the spreadsheet outputs suitable data.

4. We've now designed a spreadsheet to solve the teacher's problem and we've tested it with a sample set of input data. So far the system shows "Pass" or "Fail" but we need it to show grade bands (A*–C and D or below) so we need to amend our IF formula to fit our purpose:

   =IF(J8/$J$6>0.5,"A*–C","D or below")

   We can also format the cells to add impact and value, for example, by changing font, colour or cell background, adding borders, adjusting column widths etc.

   We also need to check the spreadsheet works with more data, with extra columns (for extra tasks) and with hidden columns. Working on these aspects might produce something like the spreadsheet shown.

5. Macros could be set up to automatically transfer set-up data into the relevant cells in other sheets.

   Try to think of other functions that could be useful to a teacher using this spreadsheet. Some examples are listed below:

   - A graph of the results. Talk to teachers to find out what sort of graph they would prefer and what they would like it to display.
   - Data could be sorted so the student with the highest mark is at the top, or alphabetically in order of students' surnames.
   - Other "What If..." models could also be created for other purposes.
   - The spreadsheet could be automated, for example, as shown on this data input screen.

1

	A	B	C	D	E	F	G	H	I	J
1	**Mark Sheet**									
2	**Subject**	**Teacher**	**Year**	**Session**	**Group**					
3	**Name**	**Section A**		**Section B**		**Project 1**		**Grade**		
4										

2

	A	B	C	D	E	F	G	H	I	J	K
1	**Mark sheet for Teacher: Subject, Session, Group, Year**										
2											
3		**Section A**			**Section A**	**Project 1**			**Project 1**	**Grand**	**Grade**
4	**Task**				**Total**				**Total**	**Total**	
5	**Date**										
6	**Max**				=SUM(B6:D6)				=SUMF6:H6	=E6+I6	
7	**Student**										
8					=SUM(B8:D8)				=SUMF8:H8	=E8+I8	=IF(J8/$J$6>0.5 "Pass", "Fail")
9											

3

	A	B	C	D	E	F	G	H	I	J	K
4	**Task**	intro			**Total**				**Total**	**Total**	
5	**Date**	15 Sept									
6	**Max**	20			20				0	20	
7	**Student**										
8	Bartholomew, Amanda	13			13				0	13	Pass
9	Oswald, Alan	10			10				0	10	Fail
10	Piper, Clarissa	7			7				0	7	Fail

4

	A	B	C	D	E	F	G	H	I	J	K
1	**Mark sheet for Annabelle Goode: PE, Form C, Year 11**										
2											
3		**Section A**			**Section A**	**Project 1**			**Project 1**	**Grand**	**Grade**
4	**Task**	intro			**Total**				**Total**	**Total**	
5	**Date**	15 Sept	22 Sept	29 Sept		15 Sept	22 Sept	29 Sept			
6	**Max**	20	50	20	90	20	20		40	130	
7	**Student**										
8	Bartholomew, Amanda	13	43	15	71	16	18		34	105	A*-C
9	Oswald, Alan	10	27	13	50	11	20		31	81	A*-C
10	Piper, Clarissa	7	19	11	37	11	13		24	61	D or below
11	Rahman, Candace	15	47	17	79	13	17		30	109	A*-C
12	Scott, Barry	14	39	17	70	14	15		29	99	A*-C
13	Terry, James	9	33	12	54	16	15		31	85	A*-C
14											

5

	A	B	C
1			
2		**Mark sheet for Annabelle Goode: PE, Form C, Year 11**	
3			
4		Welcome! Today is 30 October 2005	
5			
6		Please enter your password	
7		Please enter the group you want	
8		Please enter the subject you want	
9			
10		What do you want to do?	
11			

Models

These two pages cover...

- **modelling and simulation**
- **types of models and simulators**
- **virtual reality**
- **reasons why people use models**

Models can represent anything from machines to situations. They allow us to test how something will behave in different circumstances. All models depend on 'rules' which the software applies to the various inputs in order to produce the outputs we need. A model is cheaper than the real thing and it helps us to understand the real thing. Examples of models include...

- "what if...?" models (spreadsheet models)
- simulator models
- virtual reality
- games (see page 53)

'What if...?' Models

A spreadsheet can be used to model a situation in order to work out how altering input will affect output. For example, a shop keeper may wish to work out how his/her profit would change if the price of a product is increased. By putting the increased prices of the product into a spreadsheet against the total number of products sold in a month, a formula can calculate the effect on the shop keeper's takings. This is how spreadsheets are used to model or 'simulate' systems.

flight simulator cockpit

virtual reality representation of the view from the cockpit

Examples of Simulators

Flight simulators

The flight simulators used in aviation are very costly. However, they are still cheaper (and safer) than using a real plane.

A flight simulator has many computers to run it (as does a real plane). It is a perfect model of the cockpit; its screens and controls and even the views from the windows, and the way it tilts and vibrates, mirror the real thing. Pilots say they often forget it's not real so it's an excellent model.

It can be used to model rare situations, such as two engines catching fire at once, to see how the pilots cope.

There are far cheaper flight simulators – you can buy software for your PC for less than £50 to use with a joystick or game pad. Games like these are lower-quality models of real life.

Wind tunnels

A wind tunnel is a well known system used to model (test) wind flow around new buildings and vehicles at the design stage. A model of what is being designed is placed in the tunnel and a huge fan is switched on to see what happens.

Wind tunnels are very costly and have largely been replaced with cheaper computer simulations which are almost as good and simpler to work with.

Virtual Reality

Virtual means 'unreal, but seeming real', like your image in a mirror. As with a flight simulator, a virtual reality package combines special hardware with simulation software to produce very realistic effects.

The outputs aren't just on screen; they appeal to other senses. For example you can wear a special headset which gives you a 3-D view of the virtual world you're in; the view depends on how your head and eyes move. You can wear a 'data glove' which senses where your hand and fingers are all the time so you can 'touch' a virtual object.

The virtual world can include other people; their images are called 'avatars'. Virtual reality is very advanced modelling.

Advantages of Models

- **Models are cheaper than real life versions** because they're 'non-destructive', built on a smaller scale and use cheaper hardware.

- **Models are simpler to work with than real life versions** because there are fewer inputs to change and fewer outputs to check (each situation can be tested individually).

People Use Models...

- where real life would not be safe, e.g. inside a nuclear reactor, in science experiments
- where real life is very slow, e.g. changing interest rates, development of a town
- where real life is very fast, e.g. a car crash, the effect of spin while throwing a ball
- where the situation occurs rarely in real life or has yet to occur, e.g. volcano eruptions, weather phenomena.

Measurement

These two pages cover...

- **sensors and their uses**
- **interfaces**
- **data logging and examples**

A sensor is a device that measures, or reacts to, some aspect of its environment (such as noise level) and outputs a matching electric current in response.

Sensors are cheap and have lots of uses: in simple information systems of their own; as input units for computers; as part of robotic (control) systems.

There are sensors to measure just about anything that can be measured:
- **light level (brightness)** – the sensor is a kind of photo cell, used for automatic lighting control, alarms etc.
- **noise (sound) level** – the sensor is a microphone (which converts sound waves to a current). Noise meters and disco effects depend on this type of sensor.
- **temperature** – the sensor is an electronic thermometer, as in heating controls.

Here are some other types of sensors you need to know about:
- **digital cameras (still and video)** – based on complex light-sensitive chips, able to sense and measure brightness and colour all over a scene.
- **strain** – used in earthquake sensors, weight machines and crowded lift alarms.
- **pressure** – a kind of strain sensor that detects 'touch', common in alarm systems.
- **infra-red sensor** – to sense movement, used for example in burglar alarms.

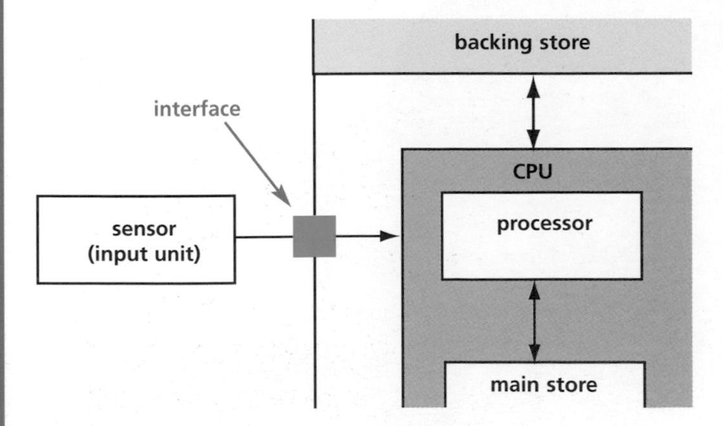

This hardware block diagram shows the interface between the input unit and the CPU

Interfaces

An interface is used to convert signals from one form to another. You can't just plug a sensor into a computer – you need an interface to convert the electric current from the sensor into data that the CPU will understand.

Data in transfer differs on the two sides of an interface. It can differ in voltage range, transfer rate and data type.

In particular sensors have analogue outputs but information systems work with digital data so a sensor's interface needs to include an analogue-to-digital converter.

Data Logging

Data logging involves the use of sensors to collect data. This can be very useful and very efficient because the sensors can take readings continuously and automatically, without the need for humans to get involved.

Data logging can also be used in situations which would be dangerous for humans. Outputs are given in whatever form the computer software package allows, e.g. as graphs or charts.

Examples of Data Logging

In school a temperature logger can be used to measure a number of things, such as the energy output of a chemical reaction, or the rise in temperature of a wall at sunrise etc.

We can take readings when we like, over as long a period of time as we like. We can process the sensor data in a range of ways such as making a table or plotting a graph.

In the workplace, sensors can be found everywhere and people use data logging to process and present the data from the sensors in the best ways.

For example, in a hospital, watching over a very ill patient may involve measuring breathing, blood pressure, body temperature and brain activity. Software checks each reading against what doctors think it should be, sounds an alarm if any reading is out of range, and outputs tables and graphs regularly for doctors to study.

In a power station, chemical plant or transport control room, a main display board outputs the sensor data. Staff can see 'in real time' the outputs of all kinds of sensors all over the site (e.g. temperature, pressure), watch for alarms caused by out-of-range values, and study the summary reports and graphs.

Weather stations use various weather sensors to measure rainfall, wind speed etc. A batch of data is then sent at intervals to the lab for processing.

Power station control system

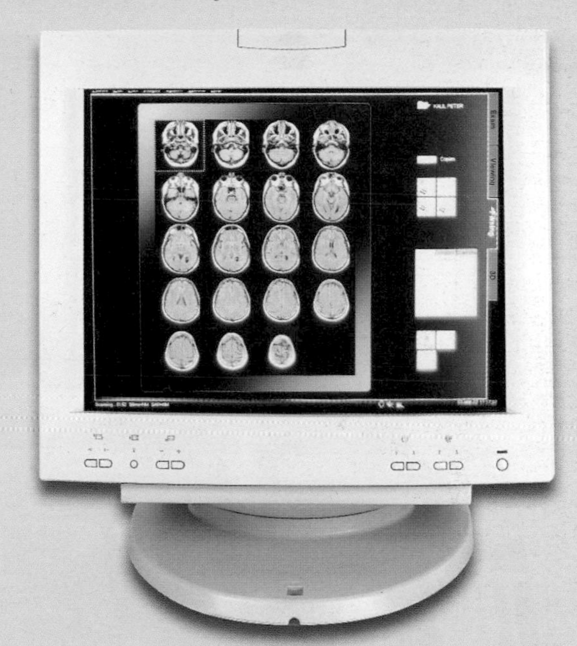

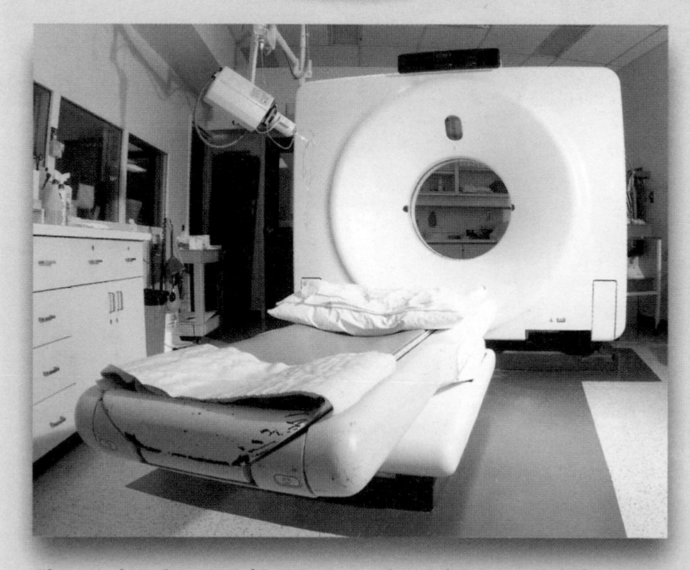

Picture showing CAT (Computerised Axial Tomography) equipment and results of a scan above

Control

These two pages cover...

- **control systems based on sensor feedback**
- **robots – CAM and the robotic arm**

Data logging (using sensors to measure and record aspects of the environment) is of great value. Sensors are cheap, able to do a wide range of tasks and can work away from any CPU and its interface, using cables or wireless connections.

There's an even more useful stage after data logging; this is using the processed data (from the sensor) to **control** the environment. 'Process control' refers to control systems used in industry and manufacturing.

Examples of Control Systems

A temperature sensor makes sure a room is at the right temperature by switching the heating on if it's too cold and switching it off if it's too warm. A simple control system like this relies on feedback – some of the output energy (from the heating) affects the temperature sensor so the software turns off the heating to prevent the room from getting too hot. This is a continuous process - a **feedback loop** (or cycle).

This diagram explains the feedback loop:

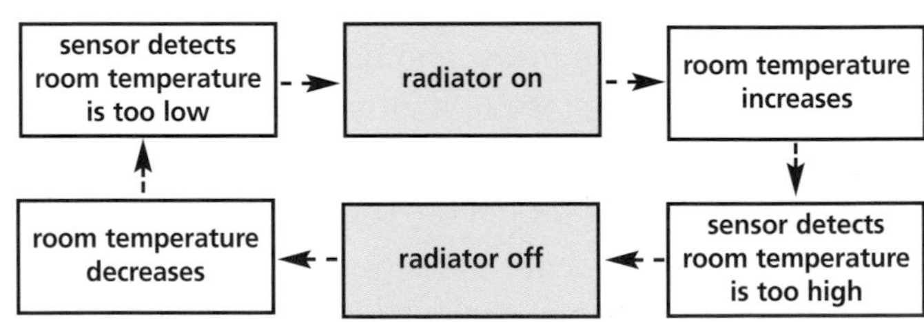

There are many control systems in daily life where control of something depends on sensor input. For example...
– where control of automatic doors opening and closing depends on the input from a pressure sensor
– where control of a lamp depends on the input from a light sensor
– where control of a bell / alarm depends on the input from a pressure sensor
– where control of a flashing 'Slow' sign on a road depends on the input from a speed sensor.

You must be able to describe control systems found in daily life in terms of input from the right kind of sensor, output to the right kind of output unit and feedback from output to input.

Robots

A robot is an information system whose inputs come from a number of sensors and whose outputs control voltage, switches, motors, pumps, valves etc; these are all things that can make parts of the robot move. A robot system is a machine whose actions depend upon program instructions and input from sensors. You need to know about two types of robot system:

1 Computer-Aided Manufacture (CAM)

While computer-aided design (CAD) is about designing, computer-aided manufacture (CAM) is about making.

The hardware for CAM is a machine tool like a lathe or cutter and the software controls its action with a program of instructions (such as from the CAD software) and inputs from various sensors.

2 The Robotic Arm

The robotic arm has joints (e.g. shoulder, elbow and wrist) and stands on a pillar (the body) which can rotate. It has a gripper (a hand) which can open and close under control of software.

Software can move the gripper anywhere within reach and turn it so it can perform tasks. For example, a robot arm can pick up a test tube and pour its contents into a beaker.

Robots are of great value where tasks involve danger, or where conditions are unfit for humans (e.g. in extreme temperatures).

You can tell a robot arm what to do using program language software (e.g. Logo), or by leading it through the actions so that it can store them in its memory and reproduce them later.

These four pages cover...

- **databases and database management programs**
- **database terms: data item, field, key field, record and table**
- **the main types of data**
- **validation and verification of input data items**
- **maintenance**
- **mail merge**
- **sorting and searching databases**
- **use of logical operators**

Using databases is one of the most important applications of ICT, at least in the workplace. It's what most ICT-based office jobs involve and no large firm could survive without its database.

Databases are used to store, process and search an organised set of related data. For example, schools use database systems for storing data about their pupils.

The database is held in backing store by a database manager (application program) which controls how the system stores data in, and transfers it to and from, the backing store and allows you to...

- view the data
- sort and process the data as you want
- change the data to keep it up to date
- run a query on (search) the data for what you want.

The diagram below shows the structure of a school database file for keeping details of pupils. It consists of a number of tables and each table has a number of records. Each record has a number of fields and the fields hold the actual items of data.

Tables in a database file link with each other, so if you need to change one detail (e.g. someone's phone number), you only need to do it once; it will automatically change everywhere it appears throughout the whole system.

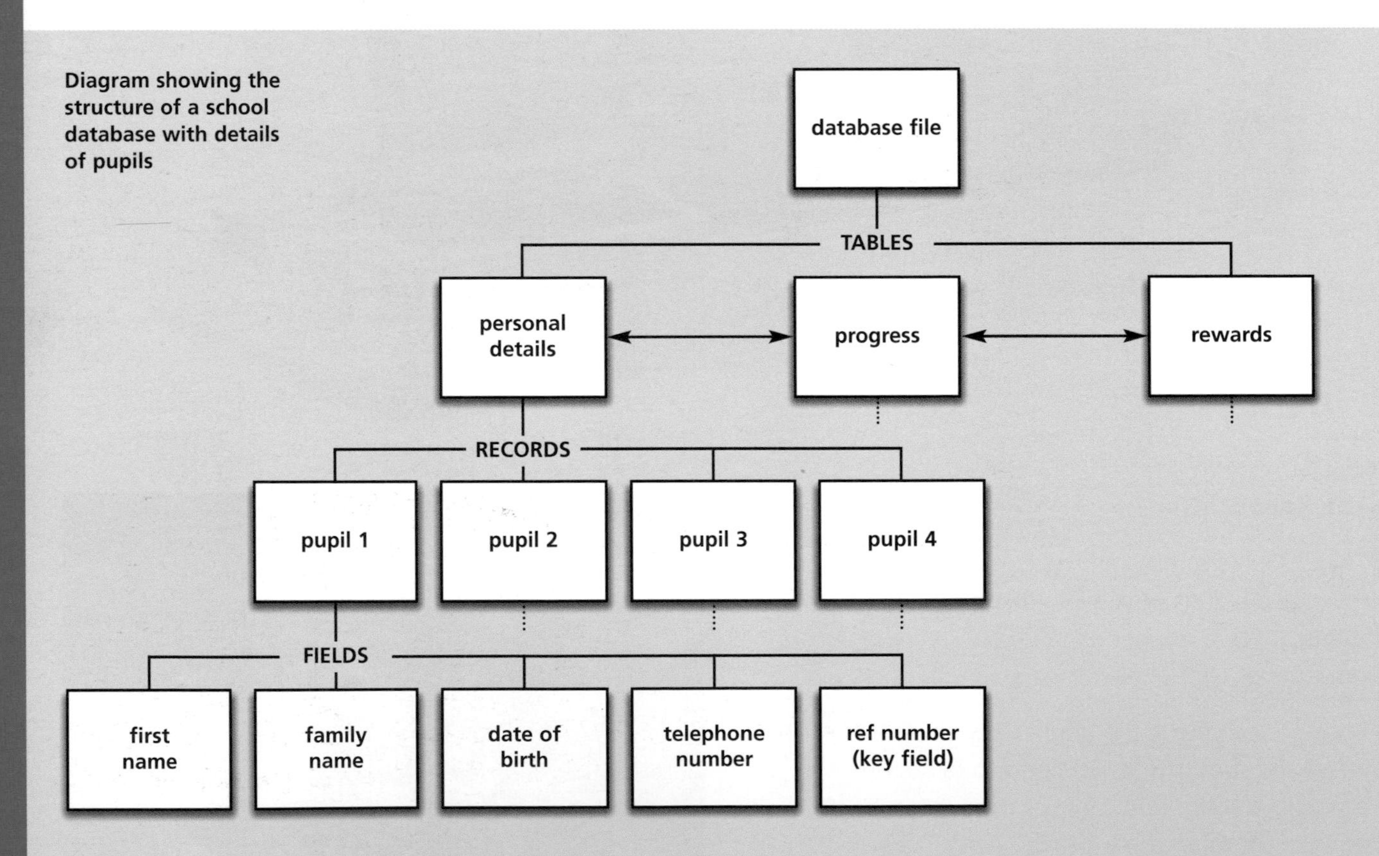

- **Field:** holds the data for one detail, e.g. date of birth, first name
- **Record:** holds all the data for one entity / thing, e.g. one pupil
- **Table:** a set of records, e.g. pupils' personal details
- **File:** one table or a set of tables, e.g. all the pupils' details (i.e. personal details, progress and rewards)

Table within a database file

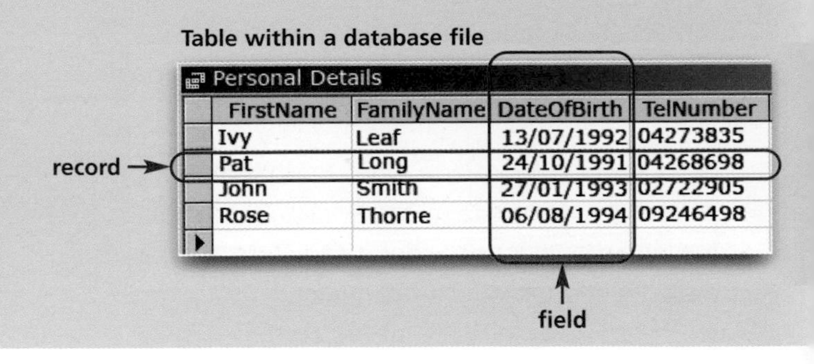

Personal Details

FirstName	FamilyName	DateOfBirth	TelNumber
Ivy	Leaf	13/07/1992	04273835
Pat	Long	24/10/1991	04268698
John	Smith	27/01/1993	02722905
Rose	Thorne	06/08/1994	09246498

Data Types and Fields

The fields in a database can contain different types of data including...

- text (e.g. surname)
- number (e.g. age)
- date (e.g. date of birth)
- logical or yes / no (e.g. eligibility for free school meals, the only options being Yes or No – see page 68)
- picture (e.g. photo).

The database manager can format field contents to suit us and make calculations (e.g. which year each pupil is in according to his / her age). The manager can also plot graphs (e.g. predicted GCSE grades against SAT grades).

Key Field

In order for the database manager to perform queries (searches) on the data (e.g. finding out how many pupils are in each year) there must be at least one field that has a unique value for each record. Sometimes an additional field needs to be created that has a unique value for each record because pupils may share the same date of birth, surname or postcode. The 'key field' is the 'ref number' in the diagram on the facing page.

Field Length

Database fields can be set to a minimum or maximum length. For example, a phone number field could be set to a maximum of 11 digits, as no UK phone number is longer than this. Setting field length means the database takes up less storage space and is quicker to work with. It can also help to pick up errors. But it can be a problem if the user needs to enter more data than the space allows (e.g. phone numbers of pupils from other countries may be longer than 11 digits). Setting field length needs careful thought and planning.

Validation and Verification

Validation is when the software automatically checks the data as it is input into the system (see page 67).

There may still be errors in input data that the computer accepts at the validation stage. For example, if the name 'Lesley' needed to be input and you typed 'Leslie', the computer would accept it as it is a valid name. The only way to check for this kind of error is for a second person to type in the data as well as you. The computer then compares the two entries and if there are any discrepancies, indicates that the entry needs to be checked. This process is verification (see page 67).

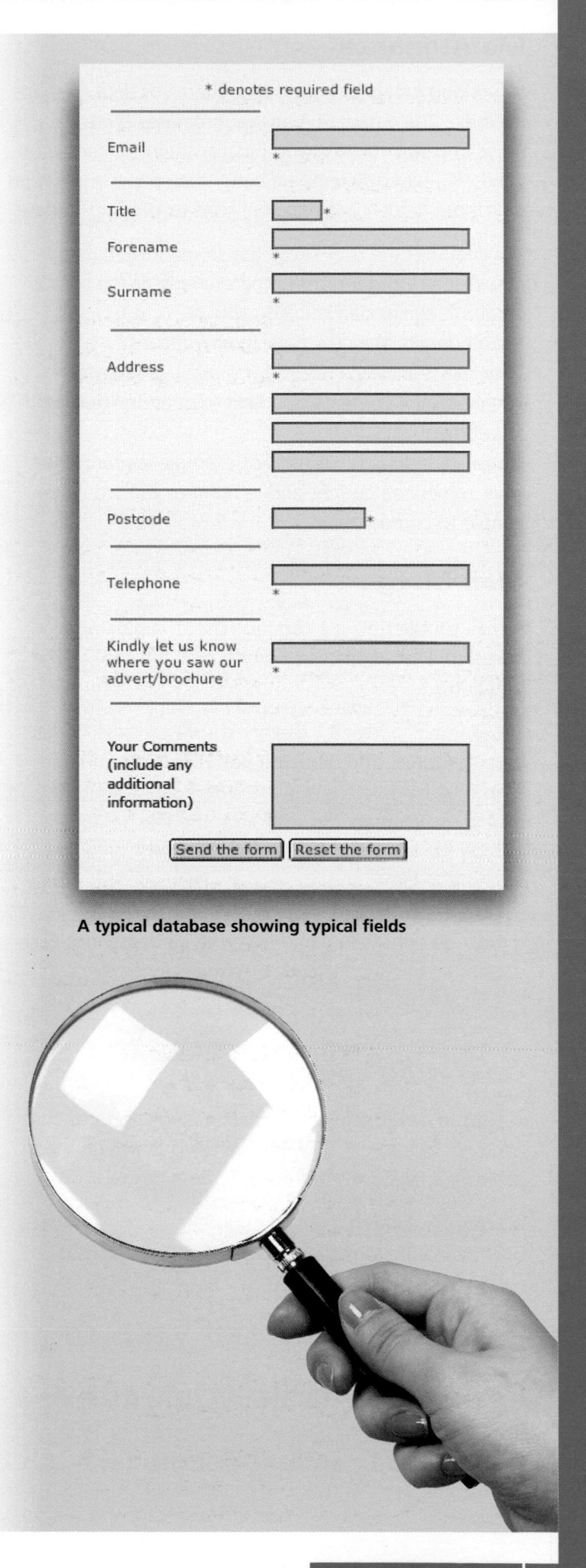

A typical database showing typical fields

Maintenance

A working database holds lots of items of data (perhaps millions). The database manager organises these data items in a way that lets you process them to meet your needs. ICT-based systems are better than paper alternatives which are hard to use and very hard to keep up-to-date.

It is vital that the user keeps the stored information in a database up-to-date. Using the example of the school database again, staff must be able to...

- add details of a new pupil (a new record)
- delete (transfer) a record for a pupil who leaves
- change the contents of a field (e.g. phone number, address)

Out-of-date data is useless. For example if you do not have someone's current phone number you would be unable to contact them.

Mail Merge

A mail shot (letter) is a common use of a database linked to a word processor which uses the mail merge function.

For example, a Year 11 teacher wishes to write to the parents / carers of pupils who have been absent more than four times in a term. The letters sent out are the mail shot. To create the mail shot, the teacher must...

- type the letter, leaving gaps for personal details like name, address and number of absences. This is the form letter.
- put the right field name from the database into each gap; firstname, postcode1, termabsences etc.
- search for the records of all Year 11 pupils (year=11) with more than four absences that term (termabsences>4), then select just the fields used in the letter from those records. This is a complex search.
- tell the system to create personalised letters with the correct item of information for each student who meets the search criteria, in each gap.

Sorting and Searching

Getting a report from the database manager about some aspect of the data is the main use of databases. You can sort data into any order you choose by sorting a field, e.g. into alphabetical order. You can then search (query) the database using a simple search on one criterion or a complex search on more than one criterion (see below) and request a soft or hard copy of the fields you want. For example, staff may want a report of predicted maths grades of all Year 11 girls against their Key Stage 3 maths levels, displayed as a table and a graph. The report could also give details of their first schools, postcodes etc. Reports can be formatted to suit purpose and audience. Data can even be linked with files in other systems.

Storing Large Files

The database manager keeps its files in backing store and only transfers the chunk of data it's going to be working with into the main store. Database files can be huge so database management often requires a large backing store that can transfer data fast. Compressed files take up less space but the system needs time to compress / decompress the data when you look up something or update it.

Operating Logically

A **simple database search** involves looking through the contents of a single field, for example, searching the postcode1 field for WS17 or typing in POSTCODE1=WS17.

A **complex search** looks through two or more fields at once using the logical operators AND, OR and NOT. For example:

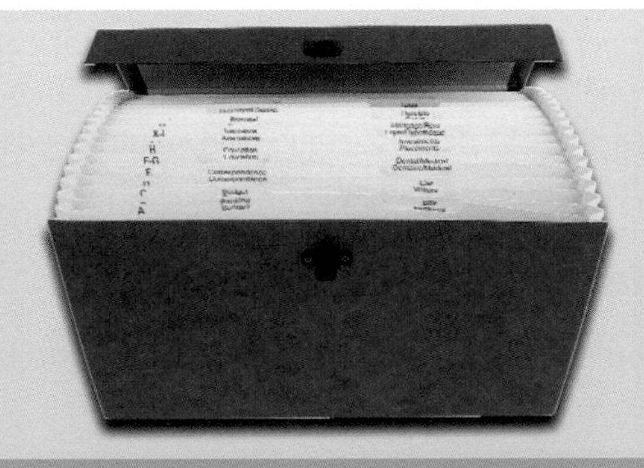

postcode1=WS17 AND year=10 ← all Year 10 pupils from the WS17 postcode area

KS3MA=6 OR KS3MA=7 OR KS3MA=8 ← all pupils working in KS3 maths levels 6, 7 or 8. This could also be written as **KS3MA>5**

NOT familyname=DEESON ← excludes people with surname 'Deeson' from the search output.

Database in Action

For a database project you would need to design the structure, create the files, search / sort the files, and get reports that are suitable for the purpose and audience.

Here is a simple version of the school pupil database mentioned previously.

1. The data table opposite shows information about four pupils from a school. A data table contains vital information that helps us to design the database. The titles of the columns in the data table give us the field names in the database (FamName, GivenName, etc.) and the data in the cells tells us what type of data will go in each field (text, number etc.).

2. This shows the type of data that can be accepted in each field. Field 4 (FreeMeals) is a logical field where the data can only be Yes or No. Field 6 (RefNo) is the key field. The key field does not always have to be number; you can specify that text data can be accepted so numbers and letters can be entered to create a unique identifier (for example, a car registration or National Insurance number). Note that Field 5 (HomeTel) is a text field, not a number field. This is because many phone numbers start with 0, which is not accepted in a number field (i.e. 01 would automatically become 1, 02 would automatically become 2 etc.).

3. As well as specifying the data type for each field we need to state the values that the system should accept and reject for each field (validation). Look at this screen shot. 'Validation rule' is where we specify the values that should be accepted and in 'Validation text' we type the warning message that will be displayed if the values entered do not fit the rule.

4. When you have designed your database you need to enter a few records to test that the validation works. This screen shot shows what happens when a date of birth is entered incorrectly. Remember that the computer can't spot all errors, for example, it would accept the family name Longe, but it is up to you to spot (verify) that this data would be invalid because the correct spelling is Long.

Once you have checked that the database works you can enter all of your records and use the system to…
- sort the records, e.g. by tutor group, age, etc.
- search for certain records, e.g. Year 10 girls with home phone numbers starting with 0427
- create and print graphs and reports.

1

FamName	GivenName	Born	FreeMeals	HomeTel	RefNo
Long	Pat	24/10/1991	No	04268698	2123
Leaf	Ivy	13/07/1992	Yes	04273835	2210
Smith	John	27/01/1993	No	02722905	3007
Thorne	Rose	06/08/1994	Yes	09246498	3101

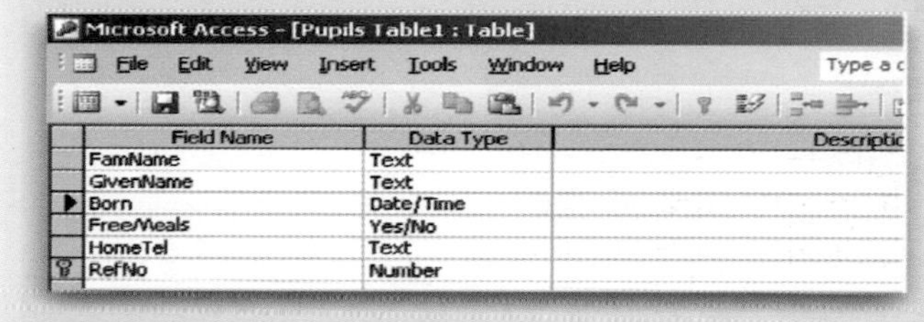

3

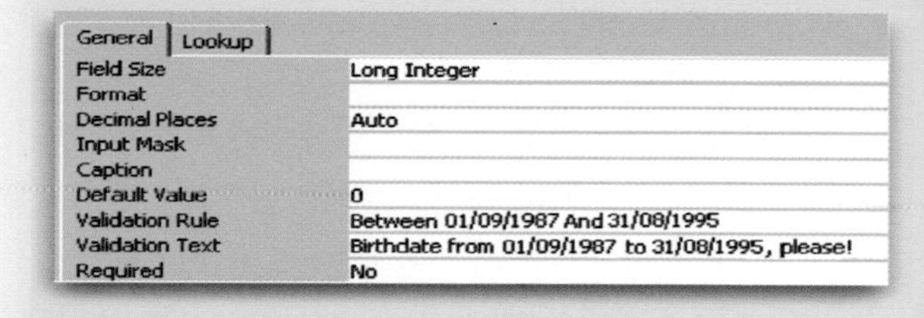

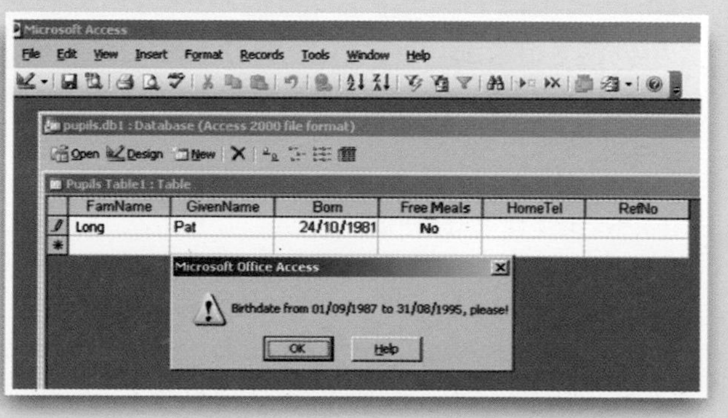

Learning with Computers

These two pages cover...

- **standard applications used in school subjects**
- **CAL**
- **other program types used to assist in learning**

We've spent a lot of time so far looking at standard (office) application programs. You should have used these in most of your school subjects; here are just a few examples of how these applications can be used in your subjects:

- **Email:** in history to share the results of research with friends
- **Internet:** in RE to carry out research
- **Word processing:** in English to type up your work (e.g. a poem)
- **Spreadsheet:** in science to record experiment results and plot graphs
- **Database manager:** in PE to organise and store team details
- **Picture processing (with photos and / or video):** in Art to process pictures for a project
- **Modelling:** in geography to explore the effect of climate change on crop growth
- **Data logging:** in design technology to monitor how a cast object cools
- **Control:** in music to create and amend sounds to mimic instruments.

You should be able to say why using a standard application (in cases such as those above) is better than not using ICT. Is is quicker? Safer? Neater? More reliable? Impossible without a computer?

Sometimes non-standard (non-office) applications and uses of ICT can assist learning in your subjects too.

The following are all examples of non-standard applications and ways of learning through ICT.

Computer-Aided Learning (CAL)

A computer-aided learning program may be just a simple science test, or it can provide you with help, keep scores or branch to a new route if the user has obvious problem areas.

CAL is also used in the workplace for training purposes.

Games

We've seen that computer games are a form of model that can be used to train and test people. There are learning games for most subjects at most levels. These include ICT-based games for learning strategies for real games like football or cricket.

Expert Systems (IKBS)

An expert system (also known as IKBS, intelligent knowledge-based system) is a kind of database that works with a vast number of rules and a large set of knowledge in a subject. Like a real teacher, it asks you questions and decides how to respond and what your weak areas are, on the basis of your answers. These systems include **virtual learning environments (VLEs)** which manage the learning of many people at once in many subjects by letting them work together via email and / or computer conference.

Sound Processing

The word processor is used mainly for text; graphics software is used for pictures; and the spreadsheet is used for numbers. The other main type of data that information systems work with is sound. You can have sound with videos and photos taken by some cameras. You can add audio notes (comments you can hear) and clips (bits of music) to documents. This has uses in many learning contexts e.g. in music, drama and DT. Sound-processing software also lets you compose and amend music and change characteristics of a piece played by a given person and instrument. These programs handle data that represents musical notes, sounds and scores (written music). So you can compose a new tune, have the software write it on screen, play it through the speakers and amend it as you wish.

Working Together

Many teachers use email as a link to their students (e.g. for getting homework in and sending back marked work). Some schools are even trying chat rooms, while a few have the students joining into group discussions via email (using the mail to group feature), or by more complex computer conferences. These are good because not everyone has to be available (on-line) at the same time, which they would need to be if they wanted to talk together by phone. Some schools have video-conference lessons for small groups.

What is System Design?

These two pages cover...

- **the four main stages of system design – the 'design cycle'**
- **the importance of feedback in the design cycle**
- **how the design cycle relates to ICT coursework**

The processes involved in the creation of an information system or software system are known as the system development life cycle, or design cycle.

You must understand the design cycle. It is an important concept because you should use this approach in your coursework and you will probably get asked a question about it in the written examination.

So how can we solve an information handling problem? Look at the diagram below which shows the four stages of the design cycle.

Stage 1: Needs assessment – identify and define the problem by assessing needs including using market research.

Stage 2: Design – come up with various solutions for the problem, and choose the best one.

Stage 3: Development, testing and implementation – develop the chosen hardware and software, test it and implement it.

Stage 4: Evaluation – make sure the new system works just as it should. Does it do the job it was designed for? Is it fit for its purpose? Could it be improved? This is a very important stage. It is at this point that we decide whether the solution is finished, or if it needs more work. If so, we go back to the beginning of the cycle and repeat the process...

Stage 1 (again): Re-define the problem if the system's not perfect (it never is!)... and the cycle begins again.

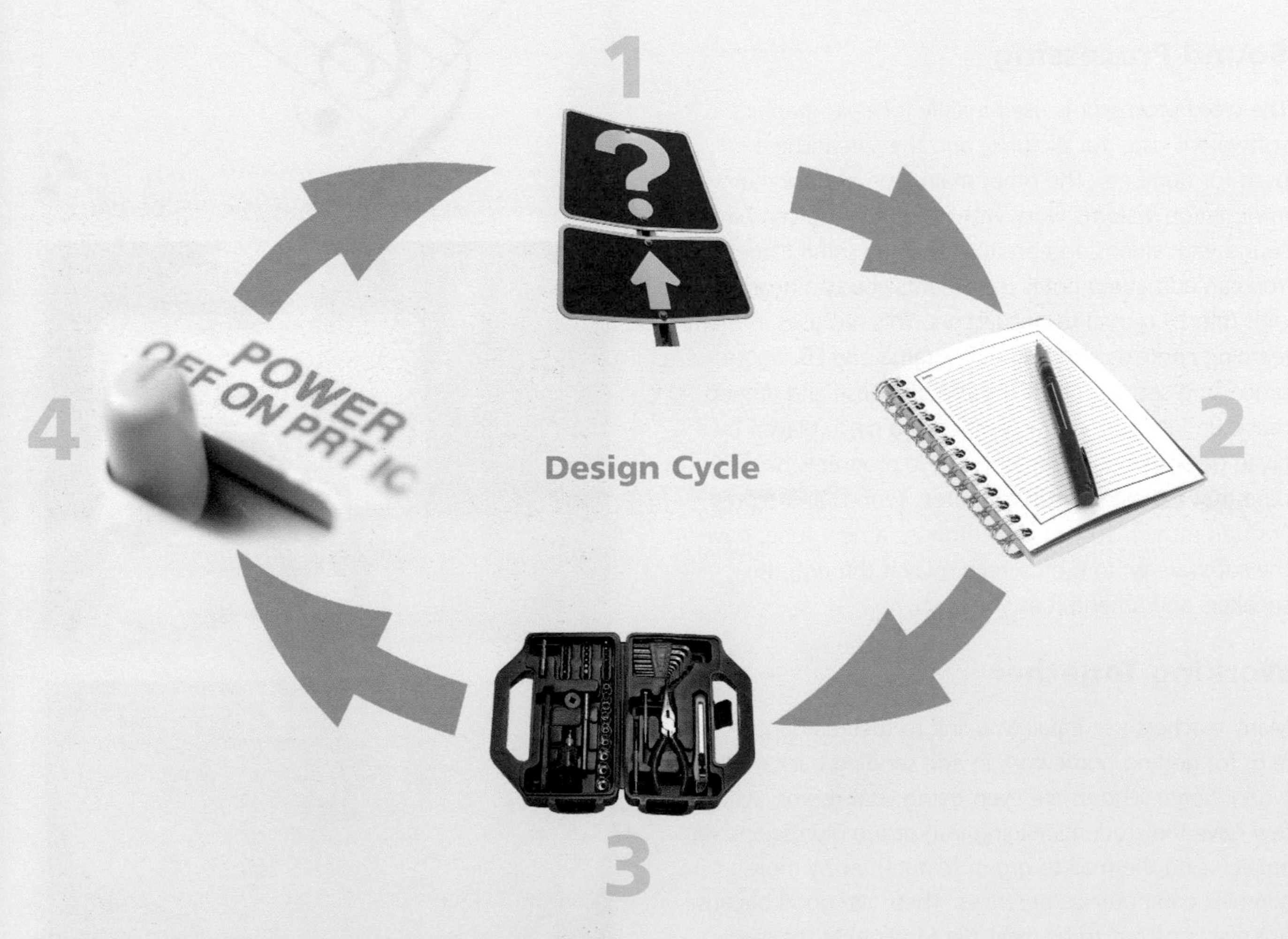

1. **Needs Assessment: what's the problem?**
2. **Design: how can we solve it?**
3. **Development, testing and implementation: develop a solution**
4. **Evaluation: does it work?**

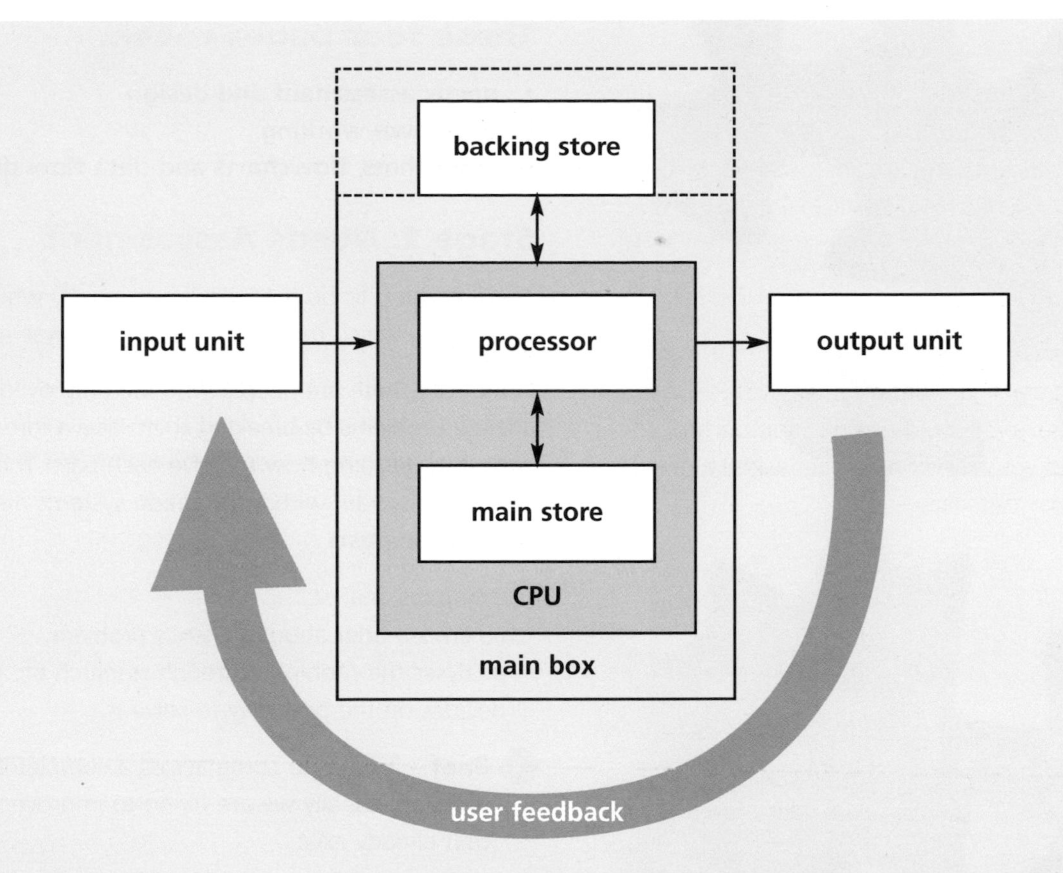

Look again at the hardware block diagram (above) and note that it now includes a feedback loop (with feedback from the user).

Feedback applies to many uses of information systems (as well as the special case of control systems – see pages 46-47). You look at the output during a task; if you decide you need to improve it, you feed that back to the input.

We can see how the design cycle and feedback cycle are used in the production of new versions of software applications. Computer firms are continually evaluating their software to identify areas that can be improved, which is why new versions with new features are produced every few years.

The starting point of any design cycle is when a problem is identified. Here is an example problem which can be solved by developing a computer program.

Problem: I can't keep track of my computer games. I lend them to friends but I don't always get them back and I forget who's got what.

The following pages will take you through the design cycle stage by stage, using the problem given as an example.

You should follow the same process for your coursework, though your teacher might give you a problem to work on and advise you how to work on it, which means you would skip the analysis stage.

These four pages cover...

- **needs assessment and design**
- **top-down working**
- **algorithms, flowcharts and data flow diagrams**

Stage 1: Needs Assessment

The first thing to do is to work out exactly what the problem is, which means we need to analyse it.

In industry there are people who are employed to analyse problems by breaking them down into separate parts and deciding how to solve each part. The people who do this work with information systems are called **systems analysts**.

The systems analyst...
- receives a brief about a client's problem
- analyses the problem (through research etc.)
- decides on the best way to solve it

1. **Brief** – It's rare to come across a completely new problem; usually we are trying to improve systems that already exist.

   You need to make sure you understand exactly what problem you are being asked to solve. In particular, you need to know the client's information input, process and output needs.

   It is important to be as clear and precise as possible about what the problem is in your needs assessment as this forms the basis of the design brief for the next stage.

2. **Analysis** – You need to study the client's current system to find out what he / she is doing at the moment, how and why he / she does these things, and how they could be improved. It's a good idea to talk to people who work with the system to find out what they think could be improved.

   It may help to study complaints and it's useful to do some market research or in-house research by talking with customers, staff and / or other people who come into contact with the system, watching them at work and using survey forms.

3. **Decision** – At the end of the needs assessment you should have a clear statement – which may include graphs and graphics – describing the current system and what the client would like it to do.

   So the outcome of stage 1 is a **design brief**.

We can now do a needs assessment for the example problem in order to create a design brief.

1. **Brief** – Client can't keep track of his computer games. Client would like to have a record of all his computer games and who he has lent them to so he doesn't lose them.
2. **Analysis** – Client currently lends games to his friends, sometimes lending each one two or three games at once, and tries to remember who has what. This system is clearly not working as he has no idea who has some of his games.

   NB. At this stage you may also include notes from discussions with other people who face the same problem to find out how they deal with it.
3. **Decision** – Client needs a system to store information about each computer game, such as title, theme, who has borrowed it and the date they borrowed it.

Once the systems analyst has identified what the problem is, the next step is to find the best way to solve it – the design stage. In industry a **systems designer** might be involved in this stage.

Stage 2: Design

The design stage is about looking for solutions that might work. You should try to think of as many different ways of solving the problem as possible and choose the one that seems most likely to solve the problem at a reasonable cost. This stage often includes a **feasibility study**, which checks if the final solution is likely to work and be within budget and the time deadline.

The outcome of stage 2 is the creation of the **specification**. This states what you will do during the next stages – how, when and why – and includes the costs for each aspect and what to expect from the final product. It should also include why you chose each part of the system and why you rejected some of the other possible solutions. It should cover hardware, software, files, inputs, outputs, processing, the user guide and the technical guide.

Top-down Working

The top-down approach to designing involves starting with the general problem and dealing with the specifics of each sub-system as you get to it. For example, you might know that you will need a database with about 10 fields and 50 records, but you don't know exactly what sort of data (e.g. text or numeric) will go in each field entry. This type of data is the next sub-system which you don't need to think about until you get to it.

The example problem is used below to demonstrate the kind of things you need to look at in the design stage to come up with a range of solutions, and develop the best one into a specification.

After coming up with various solutions to the problem, you might decide that the best solution would be to create a spreadsheet or database to hold information about the computer games so the client can easily locate them.

The specification should include:

- what hardware you will use (e.g. screen and printer) and why
- what software you will use (e.g. spreadsheet or database) and why
- the spreadsheet columns or database fields
- the information to be included in the file on the information system (inputs)
- the stages to go through to reach the file (such as data entry)
- how to sort and search the file for what you want to know (outputs)
- why you've chosen not to use other software (such as a word processor)

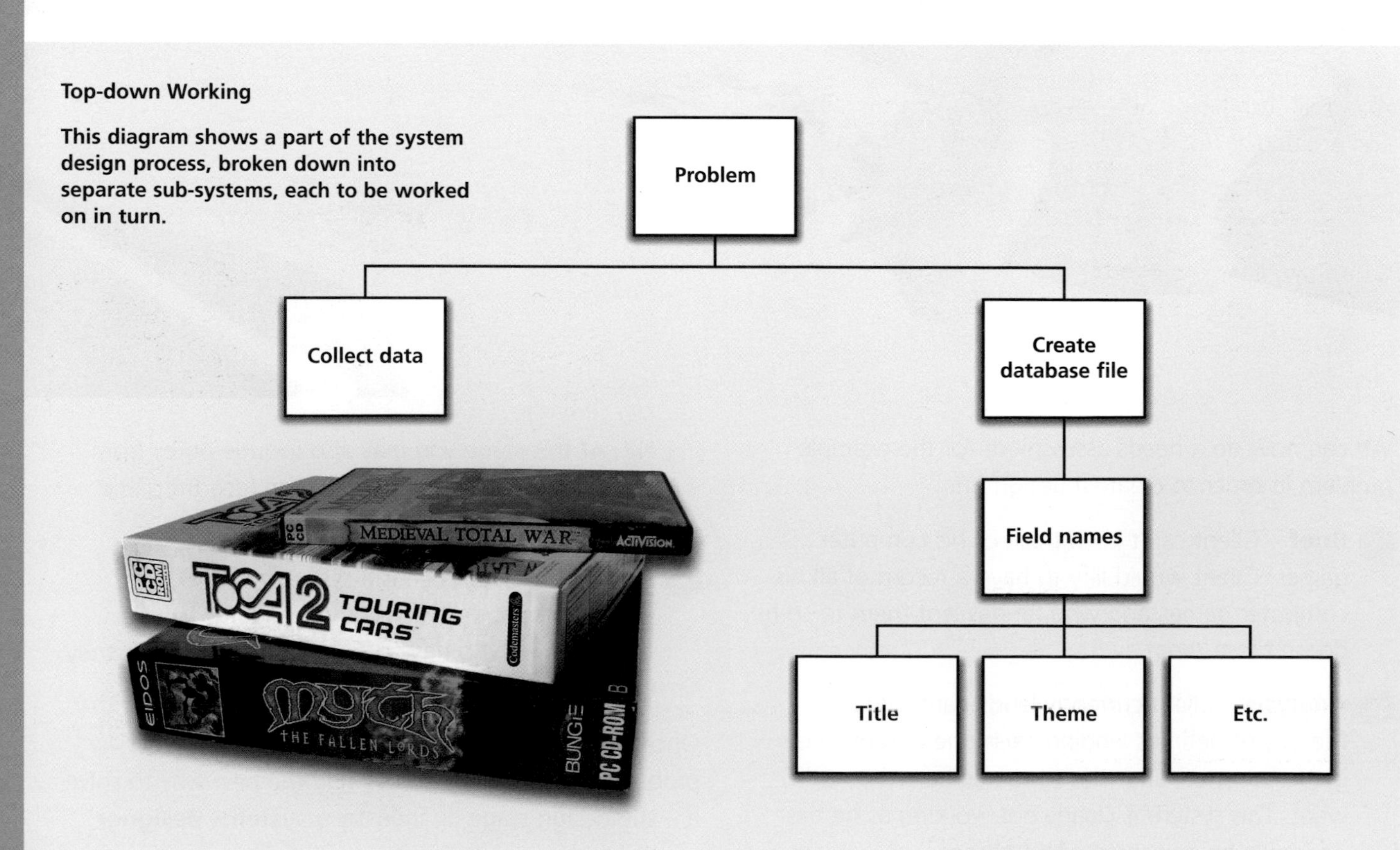

Top-down Working

This diagram shows a part of the system design process, broken down into separate sub-systems, each to be worked on in turn.

Algorithms and Flowcharts

An algorithm shows the steps you need to take in order to carry out a task. An algorithm is often presented in words, but may take the form of a flowchart.

A flowchart is a useful way to describe a system in which data flows. Systems designers use flowcharts a lot as they're easy to produce, work with, read and amend. Flowcharts have a standard set of symbols, each with its own meaning.

Flowchart Symbols

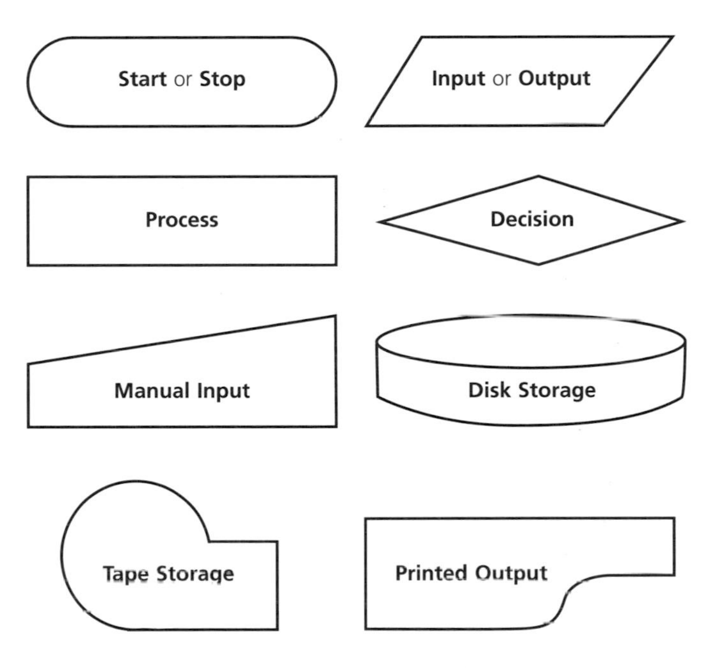

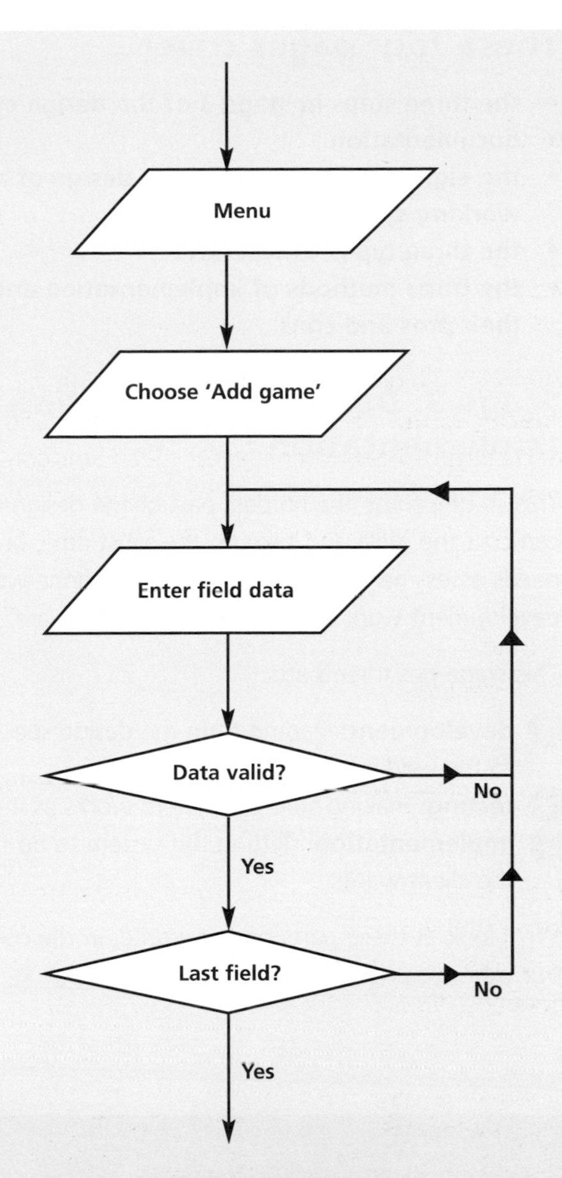

Alongside is a flowchart for entering the information into a database (part of our example).

Data Flow Diagrams

Data flow diagrams are a type of flowchart which show how the data flows through a system and what happens to it along the way.

We use the following standard set of symbols for data flow diagrams:

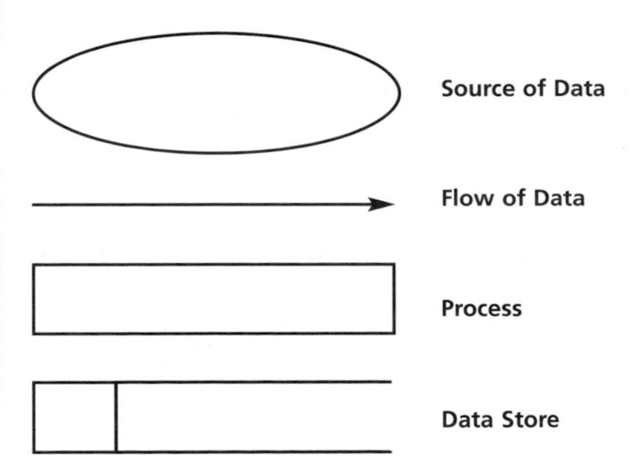

Developing, Testing & Implementing

These four pages cover...

- **the three steps in stage 3 of the design cycle**
- **documentation**
- **the eight crucial factors in the design of a working system**
- **the three types of test data**
- **the three methods of implementation and their pros and cons**

Stage 3: Development, Testing and Implementation

This stage can be the hardest part of the design cycle. It can cost the most and take up the most time, but if the needs assessment and design stages are done well, the development work can be fairly straightforward.

This stage has three parts:

1. **development:** leading from the design specification to the working system
2. **testing:** making sure the system works as it should
3. **implementation:** getting the system to do the job the client wants.

We'll look at these parts one at a time, in the context of our example problem.

1 Development

The specification produced in the design stage is only a guide. In this stage we are modifying the written specification to create a working solution.

Using a top-down approach and with a well-written specification, development should be straightforward and successful.

The specification should address eight factors:

- the hardware needed (e.g. scanner)
- the software needed (e.g. a database manager)
- one or more files to hold input data with suitable links if there is more than one (for example, to allow mail merge)
- inputs (e.g. from sensors, scanners, forms on screen, or typing)
- the process that converts input data to output data (more than one process in most cases)
- outputs (e.g. a printed report, screen display)
- a user guide that is fit for the purpose and the targeted users
- a technical guide for people like engineers who will work on the system in the future.

When designing your system, always think about the suitability of your design by continually asking yourself if it is fit for its purpose and fit for its user.

Documentation

Part of the development stage is writing guides: the user guide and the technical guide. These guides now tend to be on disk.

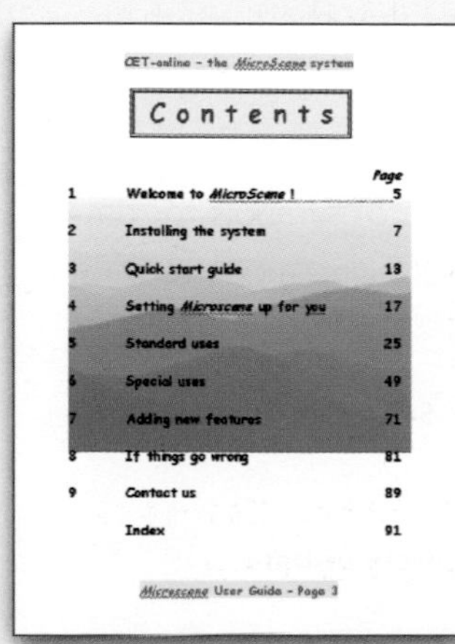

CET-online – the *MicroScene* system

Contents

		Page
1	Welcome to *MicroScene* !	5
2	Installing the system	7
3	Quick start guide	13
4	Setting *Microscene* up for you	17
5	Standard uses	25
6	Special uses	49
7	Adding new features	71
8	If things go wrong	81
9	Contact us	89
	Index	91

Microscene User Guide – Page 3

User guide: to train the system's users, answer their questions and be clear and easy to refer to.

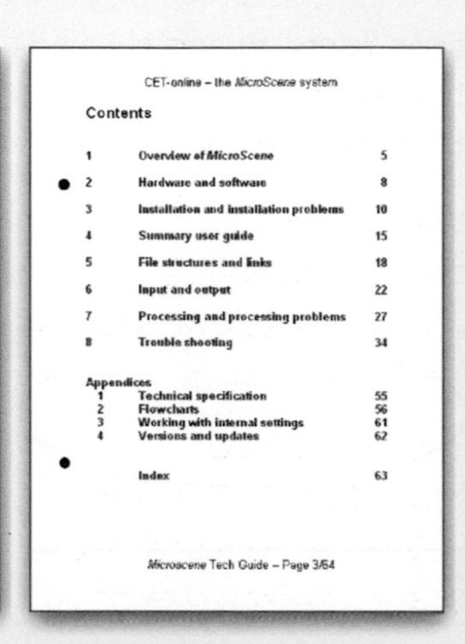

CET-online – the *MicroScene* system

Contents

1	Overview of *MicroScene*	5
2	Hardware and software	8
3	Installation and installation problems	10
4	Summary user guide	15
5	File structures and links	18
6	Input and output	22
7	Processing and processing problems	27
8	Trouble shooting	34
Appendices		
1	Technical specification	55
2	Flowcharts	56
3	Working with internal settings	61
4	Versions and updates	62
	Index	63

Microscene Tech Guide – Page 3/64

Technical guide: for experts who have to find and correct errors and update the system for new needs.

Below are the solutions you might arrive at for our example problem:

Hardware

A system like this one to manage games has no special hardware needs other than the computer itself (which the client already has).

Software

You have decided to create a database using the specification to give you the fields and the data type for each field (i.e. number, text, date, etc.). (See 1.) You must also specify the values that can be accepted. This is entered in the 'Validation Rule' box. (See 2.)

Inputs

The user will set up the system by typing details (fields) of each game (record) into the database table. (See 3.)

File(s)

Your database with the user's data is saved as a file, kept in backing store for the system to process when needed. You don't need any other files.

Process

The main data-processing tasks will be to sort the data and then run queries in order to output answers.

Outputs

These will be answers to queries such as "which games has Richard borrowed?" (see 4) and "which of my games haven't been returned?" (see 5). Design the outputs, whether on screen or on paper, to match purpose and user. Databases are far better than spreadsheets for producing different output reports.

User guide

You need to make sure the user knows how to work the system by providing clear, concise and precise instructions.

Technical guide

You need to provide a description of how the system has been designed to help an engineer fix any problems that occur.

1

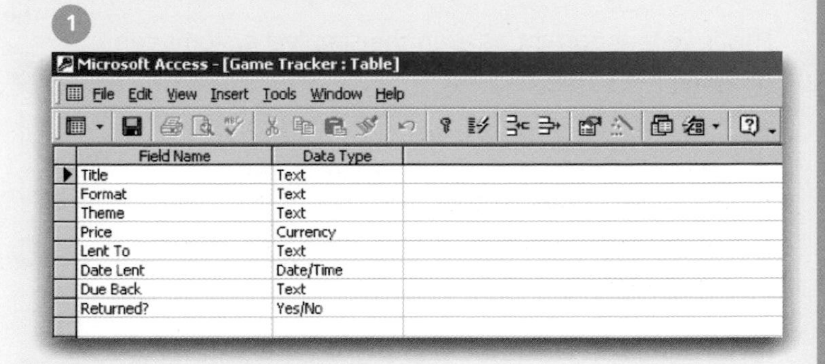

Microsoft Access - [Game Tracker : Table]

Field Name	Data Type
Title	Text
Format	Text
Theme	Text
Price	Currency
Lent To	Text
Date Lent	Date/Time
Due Back	Text
Returned?	Yes/No

2

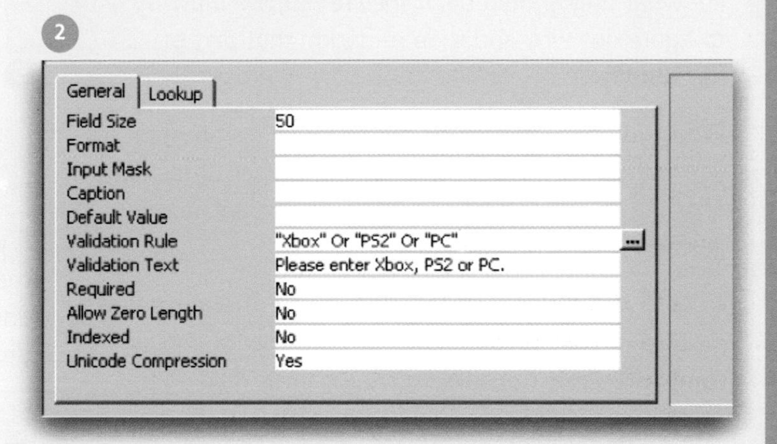

General | Lookup

Field Size	50
Format	
Input Mask	
Caption	
Default Value	
Validation Rule	"Xbox" Or "PS2" Or "PC"
Validation Text	Please enter Xbox, PS2 or PC.
Required	No
Allow Zero Length	No
Indexed	No
Unicode Compression	Yes

3

Microsoft Access - [Game Tracker : Table]

Title	Format	Theme	Price	Lent To	Date Lent	Due Back
Corpses	Xbox	Horror	£24.99	Tom	10/10/2005	25/10/2005
Dead Zombies	Xbox	Horror	£24.99	Paul	05/10/2005	15/10/2005
Olympics	Xbox	Sports	£34.99	James	05/10/2005	15/10/2005
Treasure Island	PS2	Adventure	£29.99	Jack	05/10/2005	15/10/2005
Car Chase	PS2	Driving	£9.99	Richard	02/09/2005	12/09/2005
Ice Hockey	Xbox	Sports	£24.99	Rebecca	10/10/2005	24/09/2005
Football	PS2	Sports	£39.99	Tom	10/10/2005	30/10/2005
Live Zombies	PS2	Horror	£9.99	Richard	25/09/2005	10/10/2005
Golf Tournament	PS2	Sports	£29.99	Clare	01/11/2005	11/11/2005
			£0.00			

4

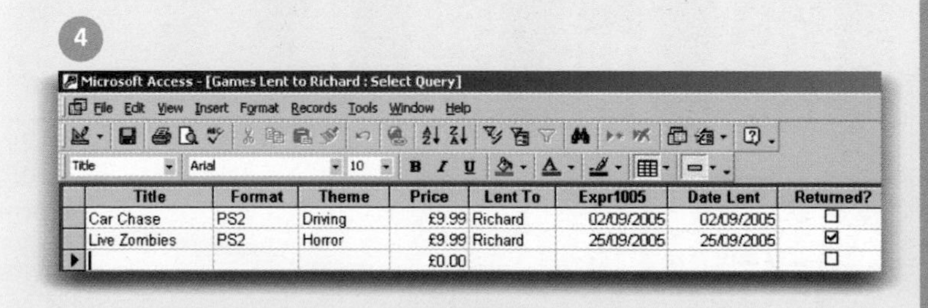

Microsoft Access - [Games Lent to Richard : Select Query]

Title	Format	Theme	Price	Lent To	Expr1005	Date Lent	Returned?
Car Chase	PS2	Driving	£9.99	Richard	02/09/2005	02/09/2005	☐
Live Zombies	PS2	Horror	£9.99	Richard	25/09/2005	25/09/2005	☑
			£0.00				☐

5

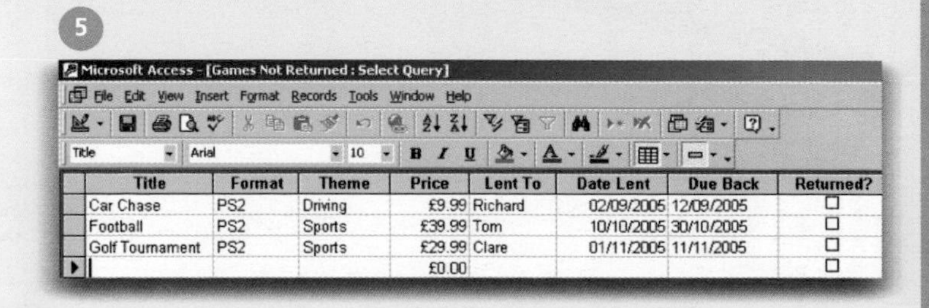

Microsoft Access - [Games Not Returned : Select Query]

Title	Format	Theme	Price	Lent To	Date Lent	Due Back	Returned?
Car Chase	PS2	Driving	£9.99	Richard	02/09/2005	12/09/2005	☐
Football	PS2	Sports	£39.99	Tom	10/10/2005	30/10/2005	☐
Golf Tournament	PS2	Sports	£29.99	Clare	01/11/2005	11/11/2005	☐
			£0.00				☐

2 Testing

This is very important as even the simplest systems can contain errors.

Too often we hear of new systems (like new handhelds or new games) that enter the market and then don't work as they should. It's better to spend a lot of time and effort trying the system out and testing it to make sure it can cope with anything users might do.

To test a system we input data and see if the outputs are what they should be. If they're not, we must try to figure out why and then re-design that part of the system.

When you have designed your system it is important for you to test the system using different types of test data. These tests will help you find out if there are any problems with your system.

To help you understand test data, think of our example problem again; imagine that the database for tracking computer games has a field for the games' loading up times in seconds.

This would be a number field formatted to accept only whole numbers between 5 and 100 seconds.

To test if the system works you should enter examples of the three types of data as follows:

1. **normal data** – data which the user knows should be accepted: in this example, a whole number from 5 to 100. Such input should be accepted and should yield the correct results when used as a search criterion.
2. **extreme data** – data in the correct format but the wrong range: whole numbers below 5 or higher than 100. Your system should bring up an error message to alert the user that such an entry is not valid.
3. **invalid data** – data that is not in the correct format. For example, decimal numbers (89.5), words (sixty) and other characters (?, £, :, etc.). Again, the system should reject the input and display an error message.

If your system accepts any data other than normal data then you need to find out exactly what the problem is and work on it until you've found a solution (back to the design cycle again!).

Screen shot 1 below shows what should happen when an invalid data entry is input. The field won't accept 'disk' because the validation rule states 'Xbox' or 'PS2' or 'PC' (see screen shot 2).

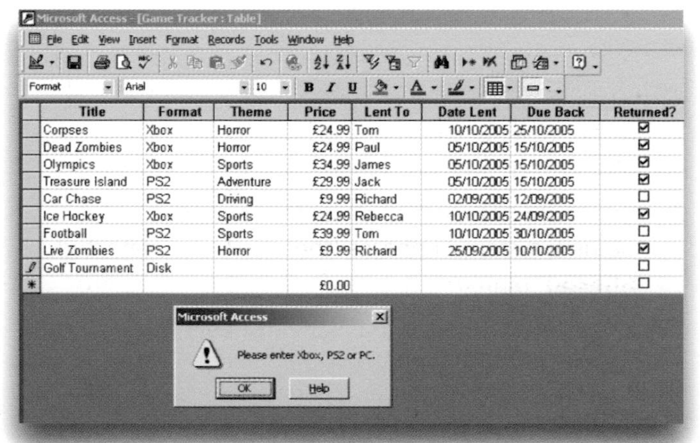

Microsoft Access - [Game Tracker : Table]

Title	Format	Theme	Price	Lent To	Date Lent	Due Back	Returned?
Corpses	Xbox	Horror	£24.99	Tom	10/10/2005	25/10/2005	☑
Dead Zombies	Xbox	Horror	£24.99	Paul	05/10/2005	15/10/2005	☑
Olympics	Xbox	Sports	£34.99	James	05/10/2005	15/10/2005	☑
Treasure Island	PS2	Adventure	£29.99	Jack	05/10/2005	15/10/2005	☑
Car Chase	PS2	Driving	£9.99	Richard	02/09/2005	12/09/2005	☐
Ice Hockey	Xbox	Sports	£24.99	Rebecca	10/10/2005	24/09/2005	☑
Football	PS2	Sports	£39.99	Tom	10/10/2005	30/10/2005	☐
Live Zombies	PS2	Horror	£9.99	Richard	25/09/2005	10/10/2005	☑
Golf Tournament	Disk						☐
			£0.00				☐

Screen shot 1

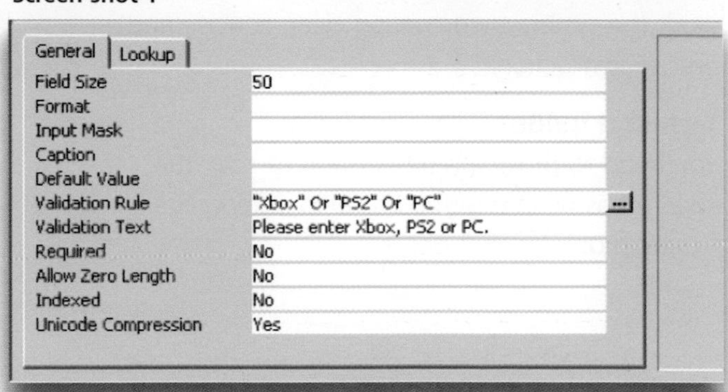

General | Lookup

Field Size	50
Format	
Input Mask	
Caption	
Default Value	
Validation Rule	"Xbox" Or "PS2" Or "PC"
Validation Text	Please enter Xbox, PS2 or PC.
Required	No
Allow Zero Length	No
Indexed	No
Unicode Compression	Yes

Screen shot 2

3 Implementation

Implementation is when the client uses the new system for real data handling.

There are three different methods of implementation: pilot, parallel running and direct changeover. Their pros and cons are listed in the table below. Choosing which method to use depends on the extent of the change (e.g. how many people it will affect) and the complexity of the new system (e.g. it may require new hardware and software).

If the new system is for a company (rather than an individual) you also need to consider the impact it will have on staff: will they be able to use the new system? Will they receive training?

When implementation begins, it is very important to watch closely for things going wrong so you can sort out problems as soon as they arise.

You will have carried out testing at the testing stage, but you cannot test for every eventuality. The implementation stage is your final chance to spot and correct any problems with the system.

Method	Pros	Cons
Pilot – using the system for a small fraction of the workload, for example, Xbox games, while using the current system for everything else, or introducing the new system in phases (the **'phased'** method).	+ safe + cheap + easy for staff + only small amount of data affected if a problem is detected + minimal stress for staff	– slow period of changeover
Parallel running – using both systems for all the data, e.g. still trying to keep track of games using the old paper-based system as well as using the new system.	+ safe + good back-up of data	– time consuming as duplicating work – hard for staff to operate on two systems at once – costly
Direct changeover – using the new system immediately and simultaneously stopping using the old system.	+ very cheap	– very risky - all new data could be lost if the system doesn't work as it should – hard for staff

Direct changeover is best for small businesses that have very good back-up of old data, but using a pilot is the most common approach because of its safety benefits.

Evaluation

These two pages cover...

- **evaluation of a working system**
- **the difference between testing and evaluation**
- **the two main aspects of the evaluation of any product**
- **evaluation criteria to compare products**

Stage 4: Evaluation

Evaluation means to assess the value of something. This is a very important part of the design process as it makes you look at the system you've designed to assess whether it...
- works
- matches the specification.

It is vital that the design fulfils both of these criteria: a system that works perfectly but that doesn't do the job it was initially designed for is about as much use as a system that doesn't work at all!

Ideally, the client will now have been using the system in their home or office for long enough to really understand its functions.

This means you can ask them questions – either in a face-to-face discussion or using a questionnaire – to find out how the system is working for them and if they have come across any problems.

Relying on the client's response is not sufficient though – you need to observe them using the system, trial it yourself and analyse print-outs or reports. Make sure you have the original specification to hand to keep your evaluation focussed.

Here are a few things you should be looking for, but these are not the only questions to ask:
- Are there any shortcomings? e.g. the company now has more customers than it anticipated and the system can't cope.
- What improvements could be made? e.g. 'Customer number' field length could be extended.
- Does it process data fast enough? e.g. searches need to yield results within 10 seconds.
- How easy is it to use?
- Is the user guide clear?
- Do the warning messages flash up when errors are being made, and are the messages clear?

We have already learnt that the design cycle is continuous – if you find a problem you need to return to the development stage to work out a way to solve it.

Then go back to the testing – does it work correctly now, or has it created another problem? And so on.

For you to stop going through the design cycle, you must be able to answer 'yes' to both of these key questions:

- 'Does it work?'
- 'Does it meet the specification?'

Remember, evaluation is not the same as testing.

Testing...	Evaluation...
is stage 3 of the design cycle	is stage 4 of the design cycle
involves sets of chosen data	uses real life data
is a short process	is a continuous process
assesses whether the system works	assesses whether the system works, is fit for purpose and if there's room for improvement

Evaluation Criteria

Evaluation criteria are measures people use to work out how well a product matches its purpose and audience.

For example, teachers use various measures to decide which textbooks are best for their work with GCSE classes. They may use a list or a scale, like those shown below, for each book.

You should be able to do the same for a designed system.

You can then add all the scores for each aspect you want to compare and get a good idea which is best.

Indeed, you can go further by weighting the main criteria – such as trebling the scores for the exam specification question as this is so important.

Is the product fit for purpose?	Is the product fit for its users?
Does the book meet the exam specification? 0 1 2 3 4 5	Is the language easy for everyone to understand? 0 1 2 3 4 5
Are the book's contents in an appropriate order? 0 1 2 3 4 5	Are the explanations clear? 0 1 2 3 4 5
Is the book up-to-date? 0 1 2 3 4 5	Are there plenty of photos and pictures? 0 1 2 3 4 5
Is the information in the book accurate? 0 1 2 3 4 5	Would the book appeal to the pupils? 0 1 2 3 4 5

Marking Coursework

Coursework is marked on much the same lines (in all subjects): the markers must evaluate each project on the basis of its fitness for purpose and users. The exam board states what the criteria are and what the weighting (number of marks) is for each criterion.

Data Input

Data Collection Form
Please fill in your responses in the spaces provided.

Surname | First name
Address
Post code | Gender M F
Telephone | Date of Birth
Medical Information

Doctor
First language | Ethnicity
Religion
Dietary needs

Please give any further details you think are relevant.

Example of a data capture form

These two pages cover...

- **data capture and data capture forms**
- **market research**
- **OCR and OMR**
- **verification and validation of input data**

Data Capture

Data capture is the process of collecting data and inputting it into the information system in a structured, organised way for processing. Data capture can be manual or automated.

Manual data capture includes...

- data entry by data-entry clerks (i.e. typing data into the computer from data capture forms like surveys)
- data from touch screens or handhelds (like those used in warehouses)
- voice input with speech recognition software.

Market Research

Market research is a method of data capture. It involves finding out as much as possible about people's views (e.g. the foods they like) and lifestyles (such as hours of work, salary).

Firms pay a lot of money for such research and they want the results quickly and without error. Details can be obtained using a range of methods including observation and interviews. The findings are logged on data capture forms (on screen or on paper).

Data Capture Forms

Data capture forms need to be carefully designed taking into account their specific purpose, who will be using them and how the information will be transferred into an information system for processing.

For example, forms often have boxes for each response, which makes it easier for someone to quickly identify the answers when entering them into a computer.

In the past, mail order and insurance firms had to process thousands of paper forms every day, and hundreds of costly data-entry clerks had to be employed to do the typing. Even now, highly automated data-handling firms still have a few data-entry staff in case things go wrong.

Automated data capture includes data from...
- sensors
- readers (data input units) for magnetic strips like those on plastic cards
- barcode readers (for barcodes like those on books)
- MICR (Magnetic Ink Character Recognition) for reading cheques
- scanners for mark reading, character reading and handwriting recognition.

The use of optical mark reading (OMR) and optical character reading (OCR) is now common as they save time and prevent errors in data input.

OCR

OCR uses a scanner and special software so that the system can read the forms. It is commonly used for the automatic transfer of written data (using 'handwriting readers') and printed data into information systems.

OMR

OMR is where machines read pen / pencil marks in certain places / boxes on forms (e.g. lottery tickets, multiple choice exams). It is a quick and cheap process, open to fewer errors than manual processing.

MICR

MICR is a similar system which has been used by banks for a long time to automate the handling of millions of cheques and paying-in slips each day.

Verification and Validation

Verification

Information systems can spot errors in input data. Inputting (typing) data written on paper forms into a computer is open to error so it's normal for two data-entry clerks, in turn, to enter the same data. The system can then tell the second clerk to check an entry when it finds that two data items, which should be the same, differ.

Validation

Validation checks are carried out by the software. The following are validation checks:
- **Type:** Is the data item of the right type? (e.g. a whole number for age)
- **Range:** Is the data in the right range? (e.g. age must be between 4 and 18 for school pupils)
- **Length:** Is the data the right length? (e.g. all British postcodes have between 5 and 7 characters)
- **Format:** Is the data in the right format? (e.g. National insurance number must be LL NN NN NN L where L = letter, N = number)
- **Parity:** Is the code correct? Items in a key field often include a **check digit**, which is an extra digit or code that is unique to each record. (e.g. 19/10/1990/A where date of birth is the key field and A is the check digit because more than one person can be born on the same date)
- **Presence:** Are all the necessary fields filled in? Certain fields can be left empty (e.g. email address) but others must always be filled in (e.g. name)
- **Table look-up:** Is the data an acceptable value within the table? e.g. data must be one of the 12 months of the year.

Even though a data item may be valid, it could still be incorrect (e.g. a mis-spelled name) so there is always a need for data-entry staff to verify data.

These two pages cover...

- **what is meant by data item**
- **data types**
- **data structures - tables**

Data Items

A data item can be a single character or a string of characters. It is the smallest unit of data that can be understood as information when processed by an information system.

In a database each field is a space for storing one data item. Even though one field may contain several words, for example, an address, it is still classed as a single data item because the individual words on their own make no sense.

Data Type

We can instruct information systems to treat different kinds of data in different ways. There are a number of data types (see also pages 37 and 49):

Text (Alpha-numeric): any string of keyboard characters, for example, a title, a postcode or even something like "2+2=4!". Information systems can't carry out much processing on text data, except for things like changing case.

Numeric: a string of numbers, like the number of pages in a book. Information systems can perform calculations with number values (as we have seen in spreadsheets). There are various types of number data items: whole numbers (integers) and real numbers. You may also come across currency and percentage as numeric data types when working with spreadsheets.

Date: may look like a number (e.g. 19102005) or it may have punctuation (e.g. 19/10/2005, 19.10.05). The difference between numeric and date data is, for example, finding the average or total of a series of dates of birth would be meaningless. But you could search for records of people with certain birth dates, sort them by date, etc.

Logical (or Boolean): can only take one of two possible values, 0 or 1. You can link any two-value information to this data type, such as gender, answers (Y or N), classifications (fact or fiction, album or single) etc. In other words, there are two options and it must be one or the other.

Holidays Query 1 : Select Query

HolidayNumbe	Location	Activity	Nights	Cost	Depatu
S002	Malaga	Windsurfing	7	249	01/
S014	Malaga	Windsurfing	7	325	02/
S025	Malaga	ParaGliding	7	350	02/
S028	Malaga	Windsurfing	7	340	05/

Database table with rows (records) and columns (fields)

D4 fx =SUM(B4:C4)

	A	B	C	D	E
1	Sales Person	April	May	Total	
2	J.Sunil	£38,650	£36,275	£74,925	
3	R.Simpson	£29,390	£34,180	£63,570	
4	D. Sands	£31,000	£32,550	£63,550	
5					
6					
7					
8					
9					
10					
11					
12					
13					
14					

Sheet1 / Sheet2 / Sheet3

spending group, 2005	amount / £
clothes	27.50
music	456.27
going out	1234.56
total	1718.33

formula: =sum(above)

Word processor table

Spreadsheet with more than one sheet

Data Structures

A data structure is an organised set of data items that an information system can handle and process as a whole (as well as dealing with the individual items). There are many kinds of data structures. One type of data structure is a table.

When we discussed database files, we noted that they contain tables. A table is something we can show as a rectangular grid of rows (records) and columns (fields), with a data item in each cell.

We can also describe a spreadsheet as a table of rows and columns. That's why it's easy to confuse the structures of a spreadsheet and a database. One way in which they differ is that a spreadsheet's rows and columns are identified by numbers and letters, while those of a database are identified by key field values and field names.

We can also create tables like the one shown above using most word processor applications. The information system can work with the whole table (perhaps to copy it or format text or borders) as well as on the cells and the data items they contain. You can also perform simple calculations with numeric data in word processor table cells using basic formulae, like the one shown.

Although word processor software will allow you to do simple formulae, spreadsheet software is much better for performing arithmetic and allows more complex formulae to be used because it is designed specifically for this purpose.

A spreadsheet also allows a third dimension to be added to the table as each spreadsheet can contain more than one worksheet (see above). Clicking on the different tabs allows you to move from one worksheet to another, for example, from one month's accounts to another.

Data Processing

These two pages cover...

- **the four main types of data processing software**
- **master files and transaction files**
- **the 'file generation' concept**
- **back-ups and archives**

Data processing takes place in the processor (ALU), a hardware unit in the CPU, under the control of operating system software and the user's application software programs. There are different ways in which data can be processed according to the software used.

Types of Data Processing Software

There are many different types of data processing software, all designed to do a specific job. Cost and speed are important considerations when designing data processing software. A client may want the results (the processed data) instantly or be prepared to wait a few hours. The table below compares the different types of data processing software.

Type of Processing Software	Speed	Used for...	Pros	Cons
Real time	instant	• aircraft control • robot control • process control	+ very quick feedback (e.g. to prevent aeroplane crashes)	– very costly – needs a CPU for each job, and spare CPUs at the ready
Interactive	fast	• games • laptop control • learning software (CAL) • booking holidays, tickets etc.	+ fast enough feedback (a few seconds' delay is OK for the contexts in which it is used)	– costly
On-line	the same as interactive, but with many users (on a network or the Internet): the central system shares its time, attention and data between all the users (sometimes called time-sharing)			
Batch	very slow	non-urgent tasks best done in batches such as... • survey results • wages / payroll • junk mail-merge • the day's transactions	+ fast enough for contexts in which it is used + very cheap once the system's set up	– needs care in setting up (an error can ruin a whole night's work)

Batch Processing

Batch data processing software needs no human instruction once it has been set running. As they do not have to wait for human input, batches are often run overnight and can process huge amounts of data.

Here are some examples of batch processes:

- scanning for, and destroying, viruses and other intruders
- making the backing store tidy for the next day (deleting files which are no longer needed, joining bits of files that have lost each other, making sure that the main files are in places that are easy for the system to get at and that the least used files are out of the way)
- printing invoices to go out the next day
- checking all the network stations are working as they should
- backing up files
- keeping the master files up-to-date.

All of these tasks, and others like them (except for printing) are **maintenance** tasks. For a big system, the tasks are automatic; for a desktop or laptop you can set them up to be automatic – but in any case they must be able to work in the background (i.e. at the same time as the user is working at the computer).

Master Files and Transaction Files

Batch processing is crucial to the success of any large firm, for example, a bank or department store. The firm's business details are in its master file, which (in the case of a mail order firm, for example) stores the records of all the clients and their orders, and all the suppliers and their supplies.

Every day many transactions take place, for example, orders being placed and new clients joining. Even if the master file is direct access, it would take too long and be too risky to update it manually each time it's used. Instead, a transaction file is created every day with details of all transactions carried out that day. Every night the firm merges the transaction file with the master file. The diagram below left illustrates this process.

In most cases the master file is serial access, not direct access. In order to find a record the information system starts with the first record and searches until it reaches the correct one. This is fine as long as the records in the master file are kept in order of key field values. So to merge the transaction file, the system must first sort it into key field order (the same order as the master file). After that, merging is trouble-free.

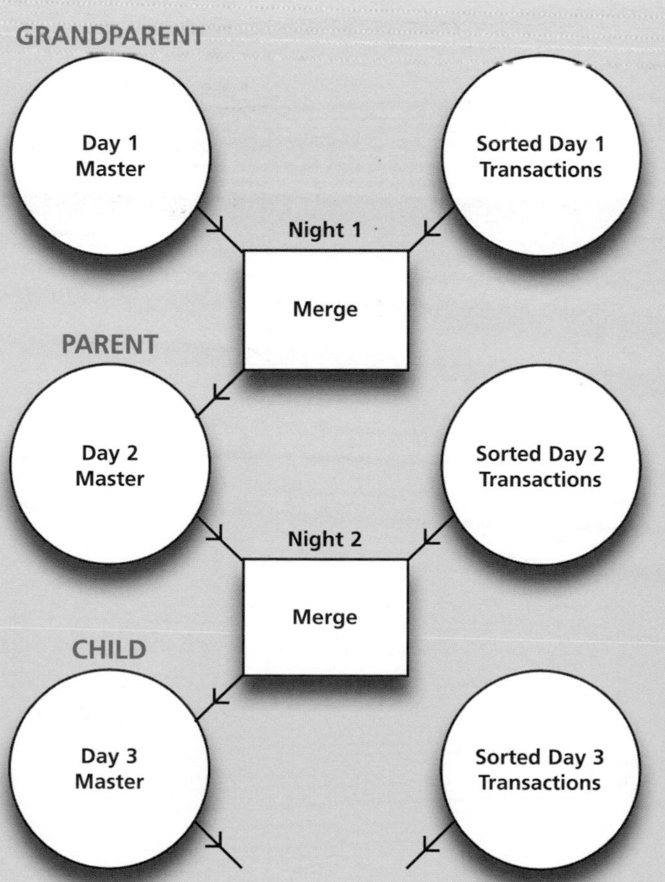

GRANDPARENT
Day 1 Master
Sorted Day 1 Transactions
Night 1
Merge
PARENT
Day 2 Master
Sorted Day 2 Transactions
Night 2
Merge
CHILD
Day 3 Master
Sorted Day 3 Transactions

File Generations

This process provides an easy, automatic way to...

- update the master file to include all record changes and transaction details
- produce back-up files.

It's crucial to store data back-ups away from the main files. Each morning the firm can store away the two files (master file and transaction file) from the day before and re-merge them if something goes wrong with the new master file. The firm could do the same thing if the master file is direct access. The file merge process makes a new master copy file and lets you keep the old one as back-up.

Back-ups and Archives

Back-ups are not the same as archives. A back-up is a short-term protective measure whereas an archive is a data copy you store away long term just in case you need it in the future, for example, if you need to refer to it if there's a dispute.

Data Output

These two pages cover...

- **the two main types of information system output**
- **soft copy and hard copy and when each should be used**
- **the design of good output screens and paper reports**

Types of Output

The two main types of information system output are...
Hard copy: output on paper (e.g. a printed report)
Soft copy: output on screen (which you can later print if you wish).

The choice between screen display (soft copy) and paper printout (hard copy) depends on...

- what you asked for (e.g. a lot of information or a little, text or video).
- what you want to do with the output (perhaps put it in a report of your own, search it for key words, forward it to someone else, etc.).
- your own personal views. For example, some people don't like to waste paper by printing everything out. Some people, on the other hand, can't grasp the essence of a document without printing it, or simply prefer to keep a paper-based filing system.
- where you are. For example someone using a laptop on a train cannot produce a hard copy in such a situation.

slide show presentation

DESIGNERS' TIPS FOR SUCCESS

- Match product to purpose
- Match product to audience
- Match product to budget
- Match medium to product

Data Presentation

The way in which you choose to present information is important as it must be suitable for its purpose and appropriate for the people who will use it.

For example, you must consider whether a screen output will be displayed to just one person (like an email) or a big audience (on a projector) – in which case the information will need to be displayed big enough for people at the back of the room to see.

The purpose of a hard copy of a presentation differs from the soft copy. The hard copy may contain more information (see alongside), so the viewers can take it away to read, or it may have space for viewers to write notes on. The soft copy, however, may simply display the main points of a subject without going into detail (see above). Unlike the hard copy though, soft copy can make good use of special effects and a soundtrack.

Always think about the following points:
- What makes a good screen output?
  Think about font size, font colour, use of images, accompanying sound track, hyperlinks etc.
- What makes a good printout?
  Think about space for notes, quantity of text etc.

accompanying handout

DESIGNERS TIPS FOR SUCCESS

Match product to purpose
- what's the product for?
- what's the problem?

Match product to audience
- who's the product for?
- whose was the initial problem?

Match product to budget
- how much could it cost?
- what can the client afford?

Match medium to product
- for an information product, paper or screen?

The way in which you choose to present information is important as it must be suitable for its purpose and appropriate for the people who will use it.

For example, you must consider whether a screen output will be displayed to just one person (like an email) or a big audience (on a projector) – in which case the information displayed will need to be big enough for people at the back of the room to see.

You can print out a presentation, but you will lose the special effects and sound track.

Our Information Society

These two pages cover...

- **The impact of information systems on lifestyle**
- **home working**
- **on-line banking, online shopping and online booking**
- **the effect of ICT on money**

1950s
televisions common in homes

1960s
phone conference

1970s
video games, satellite communications, and computerised banking and booking systems

1980s
home computers, Prestel (first internet), laptops, modern fax and computerised transport control

1990s
car computers, pocket computers, mobile phones and the modern (public) Internet

2000s
home broadband, 3-D films, and DVDs

Information systems can be found everywhere; homes, shops and offices contain televisions, central heating and air-conditioning systems, computers etc.

Email, fax, phones and computer conferences mean that there is less face-to-face communication now: people don't have to leave home or work to contact, speak to, or even see other people.

Information systems are developing all the time (see timeline alongside) and can have a huge impact on our lives.

Homes are now full of automatic information systems under micro-chip control, such as washing machines and dishwashers to help us carry out tasks, and televisions, computers and DVD players to provide us with entertainment. Many households also now own a computer with Internet connection. Internet access and using email are cheap, quick and easy; all you need is a computer and an ISP and a link between them (a phone line / modem or broadband). This allows us to do more from the comfort of our own homes.

Home Working

Advantages

- many people set up an office at home and work from there. This is called home working and is great for many professionals such as consultants and writers, because it saves time and travel expenditure
- a computer package with Internet connection is fairly cheap to buy and easy to use.

Disadvantages

- it can be lonely
- it can be expensive to set up a full office at home – other machines, e.g. fax, printer, can be expensive.

On-line Banking

Advantages

- on-line banking (i.e. banking through the Internet) lets us do things which we used to have to visit a bank or building society branch for: viewing statements, managing money, making transfers, cancelling standing orders etc.
- because we can get access to the Internet at any time we can manage our money when we want without having to leave our homes.

Disadvantages

- people are concerned about the security aspects of their bank account details being on the Internet.

On-line Shopping

Advantages

– it's easy now to shop from home over the Internet. You can browse through products, make your purchase on-line and have the product delivered to your home, meaning you don't have to leave the house at all.

Disadvantages

– some people don't like to give their credit card details over the Internet
– there's no guarantee that your purchase will ever get to you.

On-line Booking

Advantages

– booking holidays, flights, tickets for shows etc. can all be done on-line, saving you time visiting travel agents', queuing, or being put on hold on the phone.

Disadvantages

– some people don't trust Internet booking systems
– you may not get as much information as you would if you had spoken to someone.

Information Technology and Money

Developments in information technology have increased the use of 'electronic money' and reduced the need for people to handle cash.

– Workers used to be paid in cash and not many had bank accounts. Now nearly everyone has a bank account and firms pay wages directly into employees' accounts.
– Increased use of debit and credit cards means that people don't need to handle cash when paying for goods in shops. These cards have a magnetic strip on the back which is read when the card is swiped through a magnetic reader. Debit and credit cards allow transfer of money without actually handling any cash. When a customer uses a card to buy something in a shop, the customer's money is transferred from his / her bank account into the shop's account; this is **EFTPOS** (Electronic Funds Transfer at Point of Sale).
– Standing orders and direct debits enable money to be transferred into another account (your own or someone else's) without the need to handle any cash.

Our lifestyles have been altered in good and bad ways by the development of information technology. Further examples of this include...

+ wider access to information than ever before
+ a wider variety of quicker and more efficient communication systems than ever before
+ new ways to meet people (from all over the world), for example, through on-line dating agencies, chat rooms etc.
– new types of crime, for example, stealing personal and / or bank account details through the Internet, hacking into personal and business computers, sending viruses etc. (see pages 25 and 79).

New IT in the Workplace

These two pages cover...

- **the impact of new IT on office work**
- **how ICT affects working lives in other sectors**
- **concerns about the impact of ICT on society**

You need to be able to discuss the impact that widespread cheap information systems have had on the world of work. You should have ideas on how and why society is changing and whether the changes are good or bad.

Over the last few decades, many jobs have been lost in traditional industries where manual labour is required. At the same time, though, many new jobs have been created with the continued development of IT. Now computers are used in some way in almost all industries. For example, shop assistants use barcode readers, architects use CAD, most large companies use databases and factories use computers to control robots which do the work of a number of people. Using IT and computers has, in most cases, made processes quicker, cheaper and more efficient. Individuals and companies will not invest in new systems unless they will save money and / or increase profit. The diagram below left shows the stages in any process (i.e. input – process – output) and how raising efficiency would cut waste.

support resources

raw info input

process

waste products

by-products

wanted info output

New IT in the Office

When computers first became common, people feared they'd put millions of office workers out of their jobs as computers were developed that could carry out the work of many people.

Computers did do away with many jobs, but it was a gradual process and most people found other forms of work where they used computers, such as in offices. Such work is generally more pleasant; it lets people think more and reduces the amount of time it takes to do each task. In Britain, there are many more jobs now than there were fifty years ago. Many of the extra jobs are in offices.

When modern computers and communications technology (new IT) first became common, many people thought we would soon be working in 'paperless' offices. A **paperless office** is one where all files are electronic, rather than paper, documents. Keeping files in backing store is safer and simpler than keeping paper in filing cabinets; it's quicker and simpler to email a file than to print and post it; and it's safer and cheaper to transfer money using ICT than using cheques.

New IT in the Workplace

There are few totally paperless offices – but most offices have significantly reduced the amount of paper documents they hold in comparison to a few decades ago.

Many people also believed the **virtual office** would be much more common. They thought it'd be so easy and efficient for office staff to work at home that no-one would need to travel to work. There are thousands of people who work from home now, but they are mainly self-employed professionals like consultants. There is still a need for most workers to work in an office, e.g. to allow access to central records and advanced technology that would be too expensive to install in each worker's home.

ICT has led to changes in other areas too, for example, computers can control whole factories by using robots and IT-based process control.

Computers can control spacecraft, planes, trains, ships and cars, which is much cheaper and safer than having human drivers. Robot vacuum cleaners and lawn mowers exist, but they are far from cheap.

ICT has had an impact on many aspects of modern life. Here are some examples:

- Repetitive jobs are increasingly being done by machines, which leads to fewer jobs in certain industries and more skilled jobs in other sectors that require higher levels of education and skill than before. This is a problem for society as people with fewer qualifications find it harder to gain employment.
- Computer, phone and video conferences allow several people to 'meet' without needing to leave where they work. This saves time and money.
- Bosses can monitor what staff members use their computers for, to make sure they don't waste the firm's time and money. This makes firms more efficient but can threaten workers' privacy.
- Some people fear modern technology. Older generations often feel left behind and confused by new IT.
- Increased use of computers and IT can lead to higher stress levels as workers constantly have to learn how to operate new technologies.
- New IT means it's very easy and cheap for a UK firm to run its call centres overseas. Some people feel this is a threat to UK jobs.
- Internet firms have appeared which can trade worldwide without the need for many employees and costly buildings (e.g. eBay). Such e-commerce can be highly efficient.
- Barcodes and point-of-sale (POS) machines (e.g. electronic tills) in shops make automatic stock control easy and more efficient.
- Many people still can't afford to buy a computer and therefore can't enjoy the benefits (e.g. recruitment websites, cheap holiday sites etc.).

Protecting Data

These two pages cover...

- **how data can be lost and how to protect against data loss**
- **how to secure large IT systems**
- **the importance of back-up**

It's important to keep your data safe and secure to protect yourself because things can go wrong.

What can go wrong?

1 Physical damage from...
- magnetic fields
- water
- poor handling (or dropping!)
- extreme temperatures
- fire

You can lose data through physical damage of the system or the backing store. For example, if you dropped a laptop you might just break the screen, or you might also damage the processing unit and lose any data that has not been saved to the backing store. If the backing store is damaged you may be unable to retrieve any data from it.

It's more likely that you'll lose data by damaging your disks. They can be corrupted by magnetic fields (such as from speakers and screens). So treat your floppy disks with care: keep them in boxes and away from magnets. Water and extreme temperatures can also cause damage to your disks and to your hardware.

More and more people now use CD-ROMs or data sticks instead of floppy disks to store their information to reduce the risk of damage.

2 Criminal damage such as...
- theft
- spyware

Data theft is an issue that firms in particular must beware of. If it's ever possible for someone to switch on your computer and / or gain access to your private data, use a start-up password. **Passwords** are a standard feature of operating system software but you have to buy most other security software. Spyware killer software can be used to protect the computer from the viruses (spyware) that report information about you and your actions.

3 Internet hazards such as...
- viruses
- hackers
- phishers

Any information system linked to the Internet can suffer attack: there are predators looking out for vulnerable people and there are all kinds of ways in which people try to get at your data (and your money). Attack can be by virus, hacking or phishing (where people try to find and steal your bank account details) or from people trying to steal computer power from you.

Use firewall software as a barrier between your PC / internal network and the Internet / outside network to stop unauthorised access. Anti-virus software stops viruses (see page 25).

Keeping Large Systems Secure

People in charge of large systems and networks must take precautions to protect data, including setting up ways to monitor what users do with their computers, complex **username** and password systems, firewalls and other security software, and systems for archives and back-ups. They may also encrypt (code) data so that if someone steals it, they can't read it.

Security guards and cameras are often used by firms to prevent strangers getting into the building in the first place.

Backing Up and Archiving

Never have only one copy of data that you may want in the future; if you lose that copy you will have lost everything, for example, all your coursework, your email address book, etc. **Back up** your data frequently and put the back-up copies of the data somewhere else, such as on CD-ROMs kept well away from the computer (in case of theft or fire).

Copy files that you no longer wish to use and store them away from the computer. You can then delete the originals, clearing memory space for new files. Copies of old files are called **archive copies**.

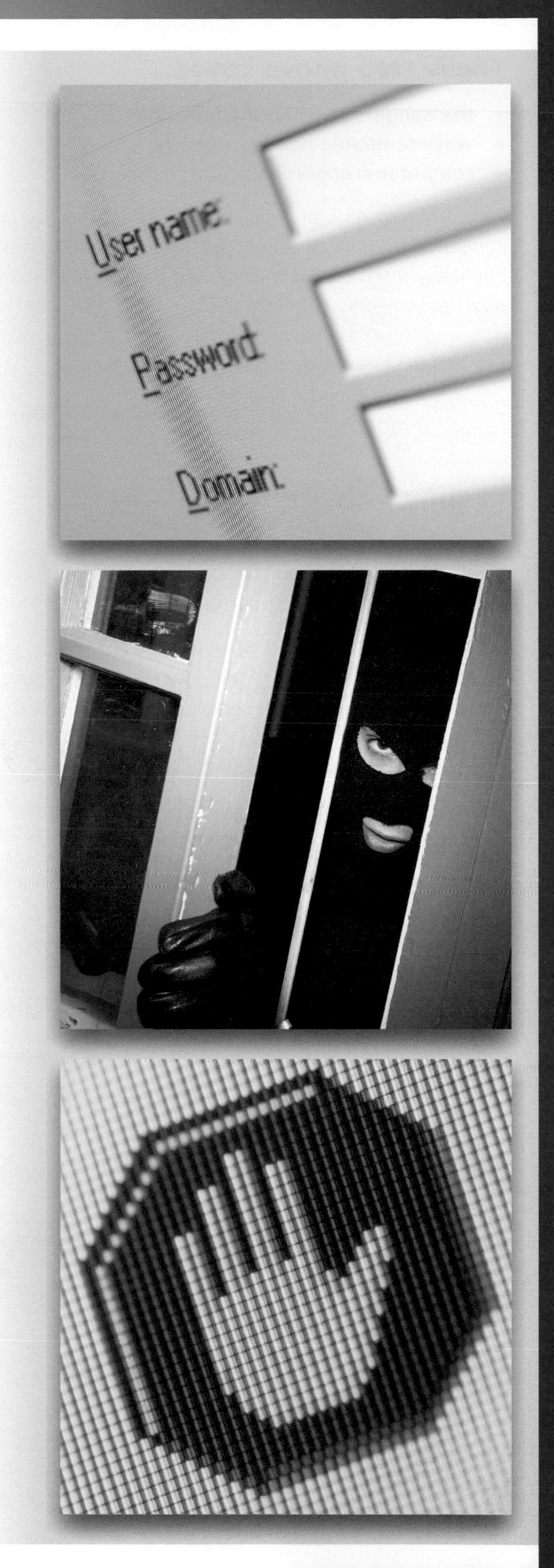

Health & Safety

These two pages cover...

- **the dangers of using the Internet**
- **ways to handle hardware safely**
- **computer ergonomics**

People who spend a lot of time (i.e. several hours a day) on computers must be aware of the health and safety issues. The relevant UK regulation (based on the EU's regulation) refers to someone who 'uses display screen equipment as a significant part of [his / her] normal work'. There are many regulations; some include rules to protect students.

But there are risks from spending even a few minutes working with ICT, particularly if you are on the Internet.

Feeling Safe On-line

Pages 78–79 look at some of the dangers to your computer data (including your bank account) from working on-line. There are personal risks too.

There are many unsuitable and undesirable websites on the Internet – the fact that some charge a great deal of money for access is a warning! But some such sites are easy to surf into without meaning to – often a simple search can bring up websites which contain unexpected material.

School and college networks bar access to such sites. They have filters which let only approved data through. You can set up home and office systems in the same way. Spam filters try to do the same with emails.

There are predators in cyberspace. Take great care when in chat rooms or sending an email to a stranger: that person may not be who they say they are.

Never give out personal details like your full name, age, address or school name, even if the stranger seems to be a friendly teenager. Filters can help with this problem too, to a certain extent.

Handling Hardware Safely

Always bear in mind that the actual information systems' hardware can be dangerous:

1. Beware of cables trailing across the floor – they are hard to see but easy to trip over.
2. Do not go inside desktop computers and TV-style displays as they contain high voltage.
3. Beware of tangles of cables on the work surface – you could knock something over.
4. Carry and stow laptops safely – a laptop falling onto someone can cause a lot of pain and injury.
5. Carry monitors carefully with both arms, screen facing your chest.
6. Make sure hardware is not near the edge of the work surface – it might fall off.

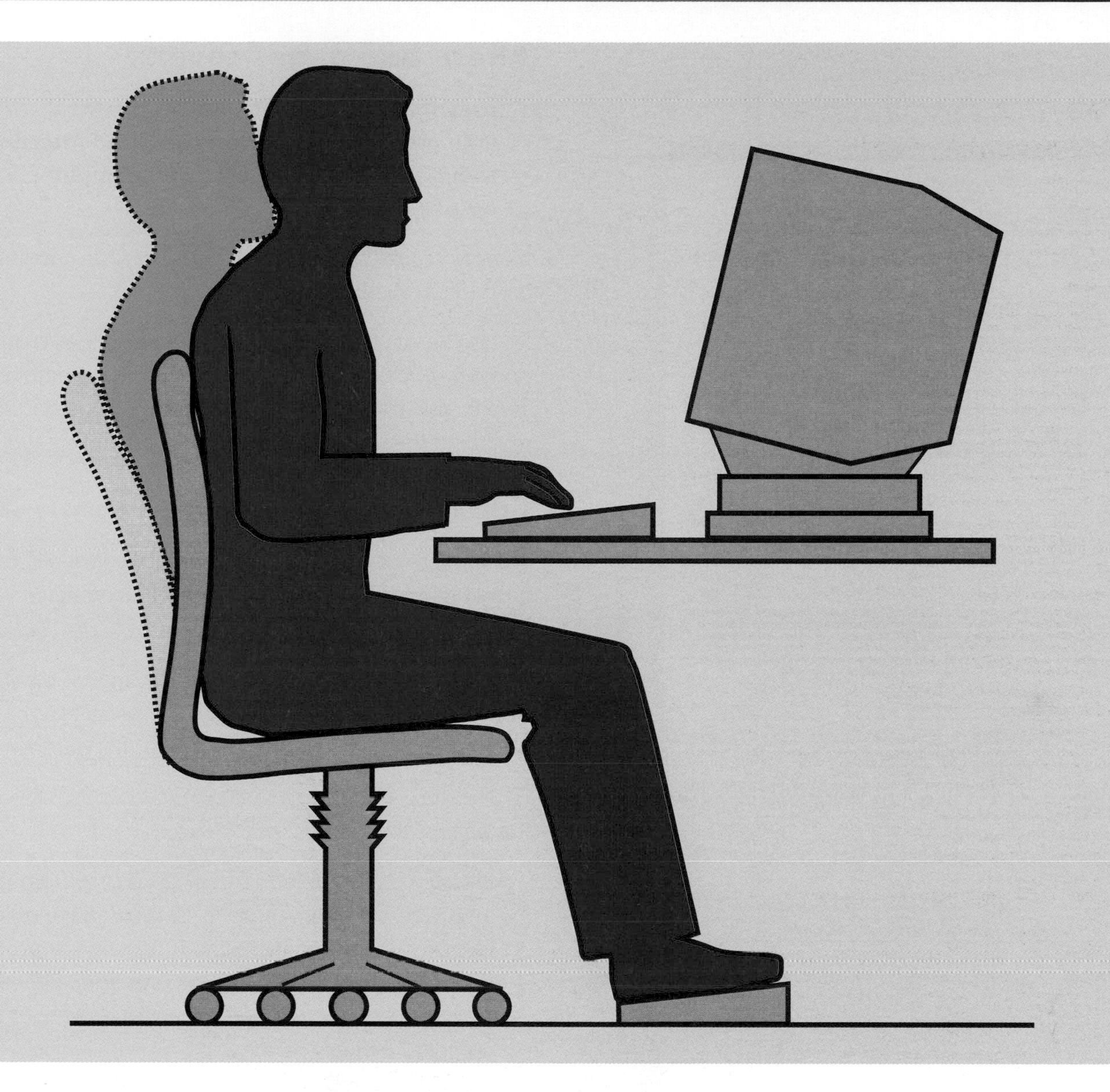

Working Safely and Comfortably with Computers

Poor ergonomics (see page 86) of ICT working areas is a big problem in many schools and colleges.

You should be able to go to any workstation and adjust the layout to suit you.

In the same way, at home, try to design your computer workplace (if you have one) so that all the users can work in comfort.

Computer Workstation Ergonomics

Furniture and Posture
- Always sit down to work at a computer
- Adjust the chair so that your feet are flat on the floor and your forearms and thighs are horizontal
- Use a chair that provides lower-back support
- Use a well-placed copy holder
- Use a wrist rest if necessary
- Workstations should be at least one metre apart so users have enough room to move

Visual
- Your eyes should be level with the top of the display screen
- Use a high contrast screen (one which is very clear)
- Use an anti-glare filter to avoid glare on the screen
- Use a separate light for non-screen work

Take regular breaks to avoid headaches, neck and back pain, stress and repetitive strain injury (RSI) in your hands / wrists.

Try to rest your eyes and exercise your legs, back, shoulders, neck, wrists and fingers as often as you can whilst seated.

If you work in an office it is your employer's responsibility to make sure that health and safety regulations are followed. If you work from home it is your own responsibility.

About OPSI | Contact Us | FAQs | Sitemap | A - Z Site Index | Accessibility

Guidance Note - Copyright and Publishing

Number: 12
First issued: 12 September 2000
(Revised 9 May 2005)

This guidance advises government departments and agencies on the appropriate copyright and publishing notices which must be featured in official publications.

Purpose

1. To explain to government departments and agencies (departments) the copyright and publishing notices which must be featured in official publications and other materials issued to the public. It also explains why such notices are necessary. Although this guidance is principally aimed at departments, other users of Crown copyright material, such as publishers, may also find it helpful.

2. We have also issued separate guidance on Notices on Government Websites.

Why are the various notices required?

3. Full and accurate notices are important because:

- it makes it clear to potential users who owns the copyright and what the arrangements are for re-using the material;
- in the case of Crown copyright, an appropriate copyright notice will confirm that the material has official status;
- it identifies cases where it is not necessary to obtain formal permission to re-use the material;
- it identifies any material that may be included in the publication that is not owned by the Crown;
- inclusion of publisher and International Standard Book Number (ISBN) details assists users and libraries to locate and order copies of published works;
- it is an opportunity to provide additional information about the material such as who wrote it, date of publication, where it can be obtained from and whether there have been earlier editions.

Which notices are required?

4. It depends very much on how the material is made available. For example, the notice on a free issue leaflet will be somewhat different to that appearing in a publication offered for sale. We have set out below four model statements that will cover most eventualities. We will be pleased to assist in producing variations of these notices. It is important that, if a document is made available in both hard copy and on a departmental or agency website, for example in PDF format, the same notices are used in both versions.

5. The notices covered in this guidance are:

A. copyright statement;

B. details of the publisher and an ISBN;

C. details of how the material may be re-used and whether specific permission in the form of a licence is necessary;

D. details of any material in which the copyright is not owned by the Crown, with the sources if known;

E. the department's website address;

F. an environmental statement;

G. reference to the Data Protection Act where required.

A. Copyright statement

6. All copyright works made by officers or servants of the Crown in the course of their duties qualify for Crown copyright protection under section 163 of the Copyright, Designs and Patents Act 1988 (CDPA88). These copyrights are owned by Her Majesty the Queen. There is no departmental copyright. It is incorrect, therefore, to refer to works produced by government as being the copyright of a specific department. Accordingly, most of the material issued by departments should include the following statement:

© Crown copyright [followed by year in which the work was first published].

7. A department may commission an individual or a non-Crown body to produce a work on its behalf and then arrange for the copyright to be assigned to the Crown. As such works are not produced by officers or servants of the Crown in the course of their duties, they are not Crown copyright within the statutory definition of the CDPA88. In order to distinguish these works we have, in consultation with our legal advisers in the Treasury Solicitor's Department, devised the following notice for works commissioned by the Crown:

© Queen's Printer and Controller of HMSO [followed by the year in which the work was first published].

and in the case of works commissioned by the Scottish Administration:

© Queen's Printer for Scotland [followed by the year in which the work was first published].

In some cases, departments may also wish to provide authorship details by adding a further line such as:

This report was prepared by * [insert the name of the author] on behalf of *[insert the name of the commissioning department]

8. For further information on copyright in works commissioned by the Crown, see Copyright in Works Commissioned by the Crown.

9. A new edition of a published work which contains substantial revisions would normally qualify as a new copyright work. For example, if a department first published a document in 1997 and subsequently revised and reissued it in 2004, the notice in the revised version would indicate the copyright date of 2004, although it would be customary - and helpful - to state that an earlier version had been issued in 1997. A reprint or new impression without any substantial changes to the text would not constitute a new copyright work.

B. Publisher details

10. It is advisable to include the name of the publisher and an ISBN in circumstances where the publications will be made available via bookshop chains, distributors and internet booksellers or sold generally. ISBNs are unique identifiers or product numbers that are invaluable when ordering publications. ISBNs also provide access to bibliographic databases, such as UKOP and the Whitaker BookBank, for which the ISBN is the main identifier. Both of these databases are used extensively throughout the booktrade and in libraries.

11. If your department does not have its own ISBN code it can obtain a unique code by contacting:

ISBN Agency
3rd Floor
Midas House
02 Goldsworth Road
Woking
Surrey
GU21 6LQ

Tel: 0870 777 8712 (9.00am to 5.00pm)
Fax: 0870 777 8714
e-mail: isbn@nielsenbookdata.co.uk
Web: www.isbn.nielsenbookdata.co.uk

Some departments may have other unique identifiers to show the series or sponsoring unit and these should also be listed to help users identify and locate publications.

12. The following notice is an example of what would be acceptable:

www.opsi.gov.uk

These two pages cover...

- **copyright and the 1989 Copyright Act**
- **data protection and the 1998 Data Protection Act**
- **computer misuse and the 1990 Computer Misuse Act**

It's against the law to steal money, personal details and so on through the use of a computer.

It's also against the law to have things such as child pornography on your computer, and the penalties can be severe. You also need to know about legal restrictions regarding the use of computers and communication.

Copyright

The purpose of copyright law around the world is to make it clear that stealing people's 'intellectual property' is illegal.

Britain's **1989 Copyright Act** protects against copying from books, using artists' work, other people's photos etc. without permission, except for your own personal use.

It is against the law to...

- include other people's text / pictures (e.g. from the Internet, scanning, friends' files, clipart libraries) in coursework, essays etc. without naming the source
- include other people's text / pictures in published places (like a school intranet magazine) without the author's / owner's permission
- copy MP3s, DVDs, CDs, software, data and manuals without permission (let alone sell the copies)
- use software and data from pirate (i.e. copied / unauthorised) CD-ROMs
- use licensed software or data on more than one machine at once (e.g. a network) unless licensed to do so
- try to pass off someone else's work as your own (e.g. material taken from the Internet). This is known as plagiarism.

As soon as you create something (e.g. take a digital photo, write an essay, design a spreadsheet for a client, compile a table of the personal details of your friends) copyright law protects it – and will do until 75 years after your death.

You do not need to add the copyright symbol (©) in the UK. If you do though, it reminds people not to use the product without acknowledging you as the source, and it's a good idea to add your name and the date, e.g. © Lonsdale November 2005.

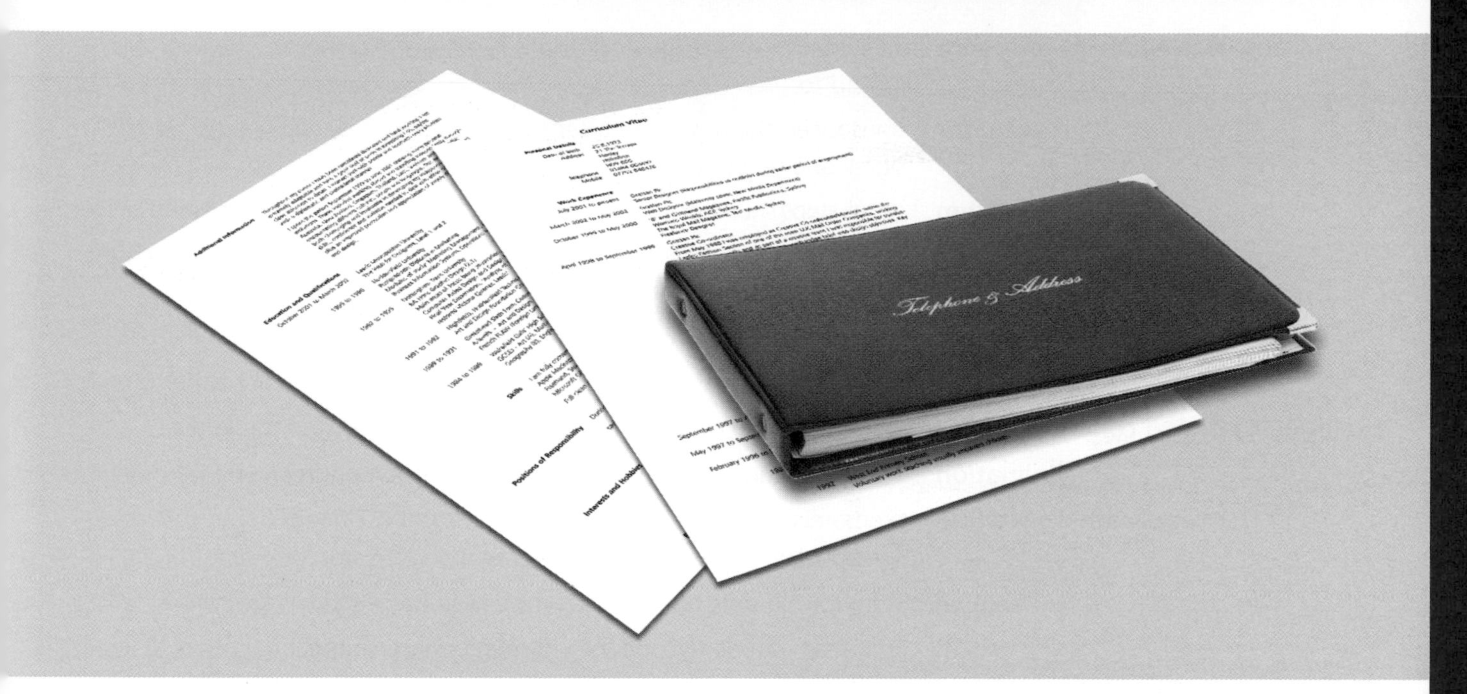

Data Protection

If you compiled a list of personal details about your friends, the list would be your intellectual property but the data would still belong to your friends. Your friends have rights too, so let's look at how to treat personal data.

Personal details or private data are called **personal data**, and the people it is about are called **data subjects**. The person or company who holds the data is called the **data user**.

The **1998 Data Protection Act** applies in almost all cases where someone holds personal data about living people who can be identified, even if the data's not in an information system (though using IT makes abuse much easier).

The law states that users must...
- obtain and process data legally
- register details of the data held and how it's being used
- keep personal data brief, secure and up-to-date
- destroy personal data when it's no longer needed
- ensure that data is not transferred to countries that do not have such strict laws
- ensure all staff know and follow the law
- provide data subjects with copies of the records about them, if requested
- correct errors when they are discovered (think what could happen with false data in store).

There are some exceptions, for example, where data is intended for...
- personal use or that of family or a household (like an address book)
- a small informal club (like school clubs and teams). Even so, we all have a duty to respect other people's privacy and to look after private information.

Computer Use and Misuse

You can use your computer to...
- keep a diary and write whatever you want in it. However, if you publish it on the Internet you need to make sure you don't include things that could cause offence or slander other people or you could get into trouble
- play games, as long as your copies are legal
- surf the Internet to find out all you can about your interests – but if you publish what you find make sure you have proper permission from the information sources.

You must not be involved in...
- **hacking** – getting into a data store to copy or change the contents
- **piracy** – copying and giving away or selling other people's software or data
- **viruses** – deliberately creating or passing on harmful programs to other people's systems.

The **1990 Computer Misuse Act** was created primarily to make computer hacking illegal. The Act protects against the following three main points:

1. Unauthorised access to computer material
2. Unauthorised access in order to commit a crime
3. Unauthorised alteration of computer material.

Glossary A-B

absolute address / reference (in spreadsheets) a reference that's fixed, never changes wherever it is moved to

actuator transducer; the reverse of a sensor; a device whose input is an electric signal and whose output is something else (like movement in a motor)

algorithm set of steps showing how to carry out a task, often in word or flowchart form

alignment how text lines up – left, right, centred or justified, there being much the same choice for text in table cells (top, centred, or bottom)

alpha-numeric term for text data, which can contain any alphabetic and / or numeric characters

analogue a continuous variable signal (unlike digital signals which are either 0 or 1)

analogue-to-digital converter (ADC) interface which changes data in transit from analogue to digital

animation moving picture, a drawing like a cartoon (not a photo)

application software program(s) designed to meet people's actual ICT needs (word processor, spreadsheet, database manager, graphics software, robot control etc.)

archive store for old data rarely used, which may be needed in the future

ASCII American Standard Code for Information Interchange; data-coding system for the 256 bytes 0000 0000 to 1111 1111, which matches each value to a keyboard character

avatar person's image in a virtual reality world

back-up copy of a file (data, document or program) made for safe-keeping away from the computer

backing store any store that isn't the main store (e.g. hard disk, floppy disk)

barcode strip of lines carrying product data that a barcode reader (e.g. a light pen) can output the data from

BASIC Beginners' All-Purpose Symbolic Instruction Code; general purpose program language (once very common)

batch process type in which the CPU receives all the data and instruction for a whole block of work and gets on with it, maybe taking all night but needing no-one to look after it

bit smallest possible piece of data (a 'binary digit'), allowed only the values 0 or 1 (i.e. off or on)

bit-mapped image form of image in an IT system in which the system holds all the details (colour and brightness) of each dot (pixel) of the image

blind (carbon) copy email feature allowing you to send an email to a group without disclosing the email addresses to the other recipients

blog computer conference (bulletin board) on a given subject which anyone can join

Boolean system using logical operators (AND, OR, NOT) to search data

bottleneck a point during data transfer when data flow becomes blocked because large quantities of data are competing for the same space

brief short but clear and complete statement of a current system and what's not working as it should be, or of the requirements of a new system

broadband channel that allows data transfer at a high rate (more than about 350 000 b/s)

browser program giving easy, personalised access to websites using their addresses

buffer store for data in transfer (e.g. on the way to a printer)

bulletin board on-line talking place, more formal than a blog, less formal than a computer conference

byte a set of eight bits, value 0000 0000 to 1111 1111

cathode ray tube (CRT) standard, large, heavy, TV-type screen

cell a) basic unit of something (the smallest box in a spreadsheet, the smallest bit of a screen image
b) as part of a mobile phone network, the area of the Earth's surface served by a single mobile phone transmitter

cellphone mobile phone that links by radio to a transmitter at the centre of each cell on the ground

central processing unit (CPU) the core of any information system – the processor (or ALU), main store (or IAS) and control unit, often on a single board, or even in a single chip

channel route for the transfer of a single stream of data, like a wire (sometimes there may be a number of channels in a wire)

chat informal message (like a simple email) you can send from, and receive at, a computer (chat room – area of the Internet where several people can share these messages)

check digit extra digit in a number that systems use to check the whole number is valid

communication a) transfer of information (knowledge) between people
b) the transfer of data between information systems

compact disc (CD) optical backing store able to hold up to 700 MB of any kind of data

complex search a search through database records based on two or more fields

compression 'squashing' data into the smallest possible number of bytes without much loss of quality, so you can store it in a small space or transfer it quickly

computer-aided design (CAD) using an information system with vector graphics and specialised input and output units (graphics pad, large flat screen and plotter) to produce a high quality design drawing

computer-aided learning (CAL) special software to help people gain knowledge, skills or understanding

computer-aided manufacture (CAM) the use of a computer control system (maybe a robot) to make something automatically

computer-readable data which is in a format that an information system can accept (read), if it has suitable hardware and software

conference meeting – with a computer conference (electronic conference, or bulletin board) people don't need to be on-line at the same time; with a phone conference and a video (camera) conference, they do

control using an information system to keep a value (e.g. room temperature) within a set range, with feedback from sensors to check

convergence the coming together of different technologies, mainly digital ones

copyright legal ways to protect intellectual products (people's ideas)

cropping trimming a picture

data information without meaning. Information systems work with data

database organised set of related data used by a person or firm to make life simpler – you can sort the data and search it for what you want

database manager program that works with files of data that relate to organised information

data capture getting data into an information system, a data capture form is designed for this purpose (on paper or on screen)

data item the smallest unit of data an information system handles as a whole, such as the contents of a given field in a database

Glossary D-F

data logging process of recording a measurement / taking a reading, using a sensor (like pressure or voltage) over time and feeding the data into an information system to process

data preparation inputting of data into an information system for further processing

data protection covered by law if the data's private and about living people you can identify

data stick storage chip in a tiny case which you can carry round

data structure a way to view data for easier use, such as a list or table

data transfer rate number of bits a channel carries per second – unit = b/s (or kb/s or Mb/s, sometimes called kHz or MHz)

data type nature of the data in (for example) a spreadsheet cell or database field, for this affects validation and how to process it (e.g. text, currency, graphic, logical and sound sample)

design cycle the stages of a process we pass through again and again to design and produce an information system

digital data which comes in a small set of values (0 or 1)

digital camera camera able to record an image in digital still or movie form for later transfer to a processor and / or output unit

digitiser input unit whose use involves changing data from analogue to digital

direct access where the system can go at once to a given record or data item rather than running through them all from the start (as with tape, which is serial access)

direct change-over stopping using an old system and starting with the new one simultaneously

disk / disc circular data-storage device (medium) – hard (rigid) or soft (floppy)

documentation information system manuals – user and technical guides

dot (matrix) printer (now rarely used) printer type

download copy (such as a file) from a large computer (host) or the Internet to a smaller one (like yours)

drive hardware that holds a tape or disk (for example) and transfers data from or to it

driver kind of utility, little bit of system software that covers the data handling needs of a single peripheral

DVD digital video / versatile disk, an optical backing store that can hold 4.7 GB of any kind of data

e-... something carried out electronically, in most cases on-line: e-banking (on-line access to accounts), e-commerce (on-line trade), e-learning (on-line courses), e-services. *(see also on-line banking and on-line booking)*

email system for sending information quickly and cheaply between people with email boxes (accounts), with various features to make it even more useful

encryption scrambling (coding) data of any type, in store or in transfer, to stop thieves making sense of it

ergonomics design of working spaces and systems to be safe and healthy for the users

evaluation working out the value of a product by checking against specification, purpose and likely users, evaluation criteria being more specific questions

expert system system of rules and a set of knowledge able to help people's learning or training as if using live expert teachers and trainers (also known as IKBS)

fax system for the transfer of data, for paper documents, through the phone network

feasibility study investigation into whether the solution to a design problem is likely to work

feedback passing some of a system's output back to the input, so the input can control the output (manual e.g. by the user, or automatic e.g. as in control systems)

field space in a database record for a single data item (like birth date). *(see also key field)*

field length the number of bytes set aside for a database field (or, if not fixed, as much as 64 kB)

file chunk of data (such as a document, spreadsheet, film, song) held in backing store with a unique name

file format the file type as shown by the three-letter code after the name (such as .doc for Word document and .jpg for a picture in the JPEG style), which help transfer and searching

filter system designed to allow some things through but not others (e.g. spam filter: software designed to allow all emails through except spam emails)

firewall software designed to protect a computer and its network from unauthorised access through outside networks, including the Internet

flowchart picture that shows a system or process through which something (e.g. data) flows

font (or type face) style of characters (e.g. Arial, Courier, Baskerville Old, Times New)

form document with spaces for people to insert items of information

form letter letter for use with mail merge with field names in the spaces for names etc.

format how something's arranged, what it's like: format of text includes font size, font type, font colour, alignment etc.

formula type of data in a spreadsheet cell that instructs the system to perform a calculation using numbers in other cells to produce the required output

frame box in a publisher program which holds text or graphics

freeware software you can install and use without payment

game model, often of value for learning and training, or for entertainment

gigabyte (GB) a thousand million bytes (1000 MB), storage for thousands of photos / half an hour of video

graphic any part of a document that isn't text, e.g. images, diagrams

graphics pad / tablet digitiser-type of input unit used by designers, who draw on it to produce vector graphics on screen

hacker someone who tries to access your machine to steal data or cause harm

handheld highly portable computer the size of a calculator or mobile

hard copy printed output from an information system

hard disk rigid disk coated with a magnetic layer for use as backing store

hardware physical, touchable part(s) of an information system

head the part of an output unit drive that does the actual data reading and / or writing

home working working from home using IT to replace mail, travel, face-to-face meetings etc.

host whoever looks after websites and email boxes, storing the data and handling data transfers, all with security

hot spot an area of a graphics object, or a section of text, that activates a function when selected. Hot spots are particularly common in multimedia applications, where selecting a hot spot can make the application display a picture, run a video, or open a new window of information

HTML HyperText Markup Language, a program language for telling computers how to work with the data that makes up a screen document or web page

hyperlink an element in an electronic document that takes you to another place in the same document or to an entirely different document, often a web page

IKBS Intelligent Knowledge-Based System, another name for expert system

image common word in ICT for a picture (line drawing, clip art, photo)

implementation moving a designed system from the testing stage to actual running – third part of the third stage in the system's life cycle

input unit unit that transfers data into an information system, based on information from a human user or data from elsewhere (e.g. digital camera, keyboard)

integrated describes applications programs designed to work well together, making life easier for the users

interactive describes software with which the human user works with little or no delay

interactive whiteboard very large screen you project computer output onto, with which you can interact to control the software (like a large touch screen)

interface link between peripheral and CPU, to change data in transit to the right form

Internet world's largest wide-area network

Internet Service Provider (ISP) provides a connection to the Internet: used by millions of users for Internet access

intranet common name for a LAN, local-area network

ISDN Integrated Services Digital Network – a costly phone-line based data network

junk mail unwanted mail, not focussed on the recipient's needs *(see spam)*

kerning adjusting the space between letters / characters

key field a field in a database containing a unique 'code' which identifies each record

kilobyte (kB) a thousand bytes (in fact 1024 of them)

LAN Local-Area Network, one whose systems are all close together, as in a school or college

light pen pen-shaped input unit with a light sensor (and often a lamp) at the tip

liquid crystal display (LCD) the main type of flat screen output unit

logging off leaving a program, network or system

logging on get into a program, network or system, usually by typing a user ID and password

logical data data able to take only one of two values *(see also yes / no)*

logical operators AND, OR and NOT, used to carry out complex searches

Logo 'logical' program language, now mainly used for the control of a 'screen turtle' to make patterns

loyalty card magnetic strip card which rewards customers by accumulating points for each purchase. Also allows shops to gather information about customers

macro a single command you make up to carry out a number of commands sequentially

magnetic media types of data storage that depend on a magnetic surface which drives can put data on ('write') and / or copy data from ('read') – mainly tapes and disks

mail merge procedure for incorporating data from a database / spreadsheet into a document

(e)mailbox space in your ISP's computer for your inward emails and any attachments

main store chip, part of a chip, or set of chips that hold(s) all data, including software, used by the processor

mainframe large, powerful, costly computer able to serve a number of computers (or workstations) at once

maintenance keeping something up to date and tidy, as in file maintenance and system maintenance

malware malicious software – some cause only mildly annoying effects, some can damage your hardware, software or files and others can allow malicious users access to your system

master file a firm's main file, for example with all the details and history of each client

megabyte (MB) a million bytes, enough data storage for a long novel or a good photo

MICR Magnetic Ink Character Reading to assist in automatic processing e.g. special characters that appear on cheques

MIDI Musical Instrument Digital Interface, system for handling data that stands for music

misuse using an information system for a wrongful act: hacking, piracy, passing on a virus

mobile a) moving
b) the common name in Britain for a cellphone; a mobile phone

modelling using software (maybe with special hardware) to make a test version of some system (a model) so we can explore how it works and how to make it most efficient and effective

modem interface (hardware unit) that sits between a computer (digital) and a phone line (analogue)

module major part of something, in this case a software program

monitor out-dated word for computer screen

multimedia data that combines text, colour, graphics, sound, video and other effects

multi-processor a system with more than one processor, possibly hundreds, working in parallel

multi-tasking when a processor shares its time between a number of tasks (like keeping a news web page up to date, watching for emails and printing letters)

multi-user describes a system used by a number of people at the same time

needs assessment first stage of the design cycle, in which the systems analyst works out what the client's problem is, leading to the design brief

network two or more linked information systems between which data transfers, as needed, under the control of software; LAN if on a small scale or WAN; three types of layout: bus, ring or star

new IT modern (post-War) computers and communications systems, based on digital electronics

numeric having a number value, one you can process by arithmetic – like 25, £25.00, 25.5%, the mean (average) of {1 3 5 7}, the sine of 30° etc.

on-line to be connected to a network (including the Internet)

on-line banking having access to your bank accounts through the Internet (therefore at any time and from any place) so you can check details and transfer money etc.

on-line booking using the Internet to book train and theatre seats, hotel rooms etc.

operating system (software) provides an information system with instructions, without which the hardware can do nothing

optical character reading (OCR) process in which software converts scanned text into data that a word processor can use, an optical character reader being the scanner

optical mark reading (OMR) process in which software guides the optical mark reader to detect marks in certain places on a page and decodes the marks

Glossary O-Q

optical media backing storage disks (like CDs and DVDs) that you can read data from, and write data to, in special drives

output unit unit or device that converts data from the system into information for the user or sends data out of the system for use elsewhere (e.g. screen, printer, speaker)

paperless office office with such efficient use of new IT there's no need for paper

parallel running trying a new system at the same time as still working with the old system

password alpha-numeric text string you must enter before you can access a system, program, website or file

peripheral any part of an information system other than the CPU

personal data private details (personal data) about living people (data subjects) held by someone else (data user)

phishing use of faked emails from 'banks' etc. to try to obtain people's account details and such

pilot trying out a new system for a small number of cases before using it for real

piracy passing on, even selling, copies of other people's software or data

pixel smallest unit (cell) of any image on screen – short for 'picture element'

plagiarism using someone else's intellectual property and claiming it as your own

plotter output device for drawings, in which one or more pens move over the paper to draw lines

point-of-sale shop checkout; where the sale actually happens; a point-of-sale system works with barcodes and credit cards to speed up the process

pointing unit / device input unit able to control the screen cursor, with buttons to give other effects (e.g. mouse, joystick)

presentation sequence of screens including text and graphics, maybe with a range of special visual effects, interaction, video, web links, sound etc., used to communicate an idea

Prestel first version of the Internet, set up in Britain in the late 1970s

process control control of an industrial process – like making electricity in a power station or working in a chemical plant – by sensing the factors that affect the process and using the data to control voltage, heaters, pumps, valves etc.

processor complex circuit in a chip (or more than one) that follows instructions in order to handle data in various ways in an information system

program complete set of software instructions (e.g. Windows, MS Word)

program language software that lets you write programs – when you run the program, the software turns all the instructions into a form the system can follow (e.g. Logo, BASIC)

programmable controlled by software instructions that you can change to suit your needs

proofreading reading through material thoroughly to check for mistakes

publisher (personal or desktop) form of word processor with page layout features

PSTN Public Switched Telephone Network; the standard landline system

qualitative data data you can't put a number value on (like your name or your photo)

quantitative data data you can put a number value on (like your age or height)

query database search

RAM read and write memory, store you can get data from and store data in (unlike ROM). RAM actually stands for 'Random Access Memory' but that is confusing as ROM is 'random access' too. Learn RAM as 'read and write memory'

random access old, misleading name for direct access (random access memory – the old, misleading name for read and write memory)

real time (in) at once, without delay

real time process with instant feedback between output and input, so the system can adjust almost at once to any change (as with a robot or the control of an oil refinery)

record space in a database file (table) for data about a single 'entity' (e.g. person, book, CD, item of stock)

repetitive strain injury (RSI) damage, sometimes severe, to a part of the body, caused by doing the same movement many times (such as when typing all day)

replication copying a formula from one cell to another in a spreadsheet

report the results of a database search, aimed at helping the user's work (output on screen or paper)

resolution measure of image quality; the number of dots or pixels that make up an image e.g. d.p.i. (dots per inch). More dots = more detail and a finer image

robot automated machine you can program to carry out a set of actions, a kind of process control

roller ball input device like an upside down mouse, with buttons for extra actions

ROM Read-Only Memory, store you can get data from but not store data in, unlike RAM

RSI Repetitive Strain Injury

satellite a spacecraft that orbits the Earth and has uses for data communication and phone usage (mainly in remote areas)

scanner input unit able to convert text and / or pictures on paper to a digital form

screen (display / monitor) output unit that shows at once what you input and the results of processing

search to look through database records for matches with what you want in a single field (such as familyname=KAUR) – a simple search, or in two or more fields *(see complex search)*

search engine program helping you look for specific information on the web with a key word / phrase

sensor device that reacts to its environment (e.g. light level or temperature) and outputs a matching (therefore analogue) electric current

serial access file type with the records in key field order: to find a record the system must work through them in turn

server computer in a network that looks after the whole network (network server) or part of its work (like Internet server for Internet access or print server for each shared printer)

shareware software created for public use; you can install and use it with only a small payment

simulation *(see modelling)*

soft copy screened output from an information system (as opposed to hard copy)

software sets of instructions telling hardware how to handle data – operating system software to run the hardware and application software to do what the user wants

Glossary S-U

sort put a set of items of data in order (like alphabetical order or descending number order)

spam unwanted 'junk' email or text / chat message

speaker actuator type of output unit, reverse of microphone

specification result of the systems analysis stage of design, the statement of what to do, when, how and why, and what the final product should be like

speech recognition software able to convert spoken data into word processor text and program instructions (for example, "cursor left three words", "new paragraph")

spreadsheet table for recording and processing (primarily numerical) data, also able to produce graphs and do some modelling

spyware type of virus that reports what you do and secret information about you

storage stick form of backing store with a storage chip in a small 'pen'

sub-system part of a larger system that has its own task

suite set of integrated application programs (like MS Office) – usually containing at least a word processor and spreadsheet program. They share data with ease – so people find them easier to learn to use

system software *(see operating system software)*

table a) way to lay out information clearly, in rows and columns (a list in two dimensions), like a spreadsheet, but also of great value in text documents b) in a database – a subset of data stored for a single purpose that consists of rows (records) and columns (fields)

technical guide information system manual for the people who work inside the hardware and software to maintain, even change, the system

teletext the data (text) part of a TV signal, like Ceefax

teleworking *(see home working)*

template blank document with the standard layout ready for use

terminal network station with little processing power of its own *(see also workstation)*

test data sets of data items chosen to test a new system for correct action. There are three types: normal, extreme and invalid

testing process of using dummy data to look for errors in a new product

text a) message like a simple email you can send between mobiles (and some laptops) b) the data type that consists of a string of keyboard characters

top down method of working, starting from a broad view, working into more and more close detail

touchpad input unit; pressure sensitive-surface, often with buttons; most commonly used on laptops in place of a mouse

transducer a) any device which converts energy from one form to a second, b) the opposite of a sensor: its output matches its electric input

Trojan (horse) malicious software disguised as a legitimate application *(see malware)*

turtle object on screen controlled by Logo programming language, through commands e.g. LEFT 45 (rotate 45° to the left)

USB Universal Serial Bus, information system socket able to transfer data at high rates

user ID the name a system knows you by, which you have to input when you log on

user interface link between an information system and its human user(s), which must be fit for the user(s) and for the purpose. There are three types: graphical, command driven and menu driven

utility small program that performs a very specific task

validation checking that an input data item is valid (e.g. your age being 180 or a postcode starting with a digit would not be valid)

VDU Visual Display Unit, commonly used to refer to a screen

vector graphics form of drawing in an IT system which stores each part of the image (line, shape, bit of shading) as a mathematical definition

verification having a second person enter the same set of data so the system can report any errors

video digitiser input unit that takes in analogue video (such as from broadcast or tape) to produce digital data

virtual learning environment (VLE) web-based learning area incorporating on-line teaching and learning materials, which is able to manage the learners and the learning resources

virtual office simulation of an office people can work inside while really working at home

virtual reality highly realistic computer-generated environment with which you can interact by way of special headset, clothing, and furniture

virus malicious software that attaches itself to another program or file so it can spread from one computer to another *(see malware)*

voice input data entry using a microphone rather than a keyboard, with speech recognition software to handle the data from the input sound waves

volatile describes a data store which needs power to retain the data

WAN Wide-Area Network, a network whose parts may be many kilometres apart

web Worldwide Web; collection of Internet sites offering multimedia, accessed through the Internet (the web is often used to refer to the Internet and vice versa) *(see Internet)*

web browser *(see browser)*

web design the design and production of web pages and web sites

web page part of a website (in most cases) a 'screen' of information

webcam very cheap digital camera with low quality still and video output

website data store on the Internet with its own, unique address

wiki type of blog but sticking to a given, fairly serious, subject (such as education), an on-line encyclopedia developed by the users; allows users to add to content

wild card symbol used in searching, such as ? for an unknown single character and * for any number of unknown characters – so searching for Sm?th* could find Smith, Smythe, Smithson and so on

wizard piece of software designed to guide you through a process e.g. using a scanner, setting up a new database

workstation machine at which a single user in a network works *(see also terminal)*

worm malicious software that can spread itself to other computers and networks *(see malware)*

yes / no another name for a logical data item

zip drive portable hard disk used as a backing store you can carry with you

Index A-F

Index P-Z